Beyond Symptom Suppression: Improving Long-Term Outcomes of Schizophrenia

Committee on Psychopathology
Group for the Advancement of Psychiatry

David A. Adler, Boston, MA, *Chairperson*
Jeffrey Berlant, Boise, ID
John P. Dochery, Nashua, NH
Robert A. Dorwart, Cambridge, MA
Robert E. Drake, Hanover, NH
James M. Ellison, Watertown, MA
Howard H. Goldman, Potomac, MD
Anthony F. Lehman, Baltimore, MD
Kathleen A. Pajer, Pittsburgh, PA
Samuel G. Siris, Glen Oaks, NY

Douglas Lehrer, Cincinnati, OH, *GAP Fellow*

Beyond Symptom Suppression: Improving Long-Term Outcomes of Schizophrenia

Formulated by the
Committee on Psychopathology

Group for the Advancement of Psychiatry

Report No. 134

Published by

American Psychiatric Press, Inc.

Washington, DC
London, England

Manufactured in the United States of America on acid-free paper
First Edition 95 94 93 92 4 3 2 1
Published by American Psychiatric Press, Inc.
1400 K Street, N.W., Washington, DC 20005

Library of Congress Cataloging-in-Publication Data

Beyond symptom suppression : improving long-term outcomes of schizophrenia / formulated by the Committee on Psychopathology, Group for the Advancement of Psychiatry.
p. cm. — (Report ; no. 134)
Includes bibliographical references and index.
ISBN 0-87318-202-2 (alk. paper)
1. Schizophrenia—Treatment. I. Group for the Advancement of Psychiatry. Committee on Psychopathology. II. Series: Group for the Advancement of Psychiatry : 1984) ; no. 134.
[DNLM: 1. Long Term Care. 2. Longitudinal Studies. 3. Schizophrenia—therapy. W1 RE209BR no. 134 / WM 203 B573]
RC321.G7 no. 134
[RC514]
616.89 s—dc20
[616.89'8206]
DNLM/DLC
for Library of Congress 91-26231
CIP

British Cataloguing in Publication Data

A CIP record is available from the British Library.

Table of Contents

Contributors

David A. Adler, M.D., Chairperson
Chief, Division of Adult Psychiatry, New England Medical Center Hospitals; Professor of Psychiatry, Tufts University School of Medicine, Boston, Massachusetts

Jeffrey Berlant, M.D., Ph.D.
Medical Director of Psychiatric Services, St. Alphoneus Regional Medical Center, Boise, Idaho

John P. Docherty, M.D.
Medical Director, Brookside Hospital, Nashua, New Hampshire; Clinical Professor of Psychiatry, Tufts University School of Medicine, Boston, Massachusetts

Robert A. Dorwart, M.D., M.P.H.
Chairman, Mental Health Policy Working Group, Kennedy School of Government, Harvard University, Cambridge, Massachusetts; Associate Professor of Psychiatry, Harvard Medical School, Boston, Massachusetts

Robert E. Drake, M.D., Ph.D.
Director, New Hampshire-Dartmouth Psychiatric Research Center; Associate Professor of Psychiatry, Dartmouth Medical School, Hanover, New Hampshire

James M. Ellison, M.D.
Assistant Professor of Psychiatry, Harvard Medical School, Boston, Massachusetts

Howard H. Goldman, M.D., Ph.D.
Director of Mental Health Policy Studies and Professor of Psychiatry, University of Maryland School of Medicine, Baltimore, Maryland

Anthony F. Lehman, M.D., M.P.H.
Director, Division of Rehabilitation Psychiatry; Associate Professor of Psychiatry, University of Maryland School of Medicine, Baltimore, Maryland

Douglas Lehrer, M.D.
GAP Fellow, Cincinnati, Ohio

Kathleen A. Pajer, M.D., M.P.H.
Co-Director, Psychiatric Residency Training Program, Assistant Professor of Psychiatry, Department of Psychiatry, University of Pittsburgh School of Medicine, Pittsburgh, Pennsylvania

Samuel G. Siris, M.D.
Director of Partial Hospitalization, Hillside Hospital, Glen Oaks, New York; Professor of Psychiatry, Albert Einstein College of Medicine, New York, New York

1

Toward a Comprehensive Approach to Schizophrenia

The diagnosis of schizophrenia has been in use for nearly 100 years, but how to care for people with this disorder is still the root of much debate and concern. Historically, the treatment approaches have changed dramatically. Policies and attitudes towards treatment, however, have swung from total pessimism in the early 1900s to naive optimism in the 1960s, and recently back to a more negative perspective on the disorder. New data that have emerged on the longitudinal course of schizophrenia suggest that the outcomes for this disorder may be less bleak than originally feared. Examination of these data also suggest directions for changes in our current perspectives toward the care of these patients. In this chapter, we will summarize the care and treatment of people with schizophrenia as it has evolved over this century and then briefly review the results of the longitudinal studies of the disorder. This review will serve as the basis for proposing a new approach to schizophrenia, one that integrates features of both chronic institutional care and acute suppression of symptoms.

Historical Background

A number of factors have contributed to the vacillations in our profession's approaches to individuals with schizophrenia. The first is the history of the nosology of the disorder. The syndrome was originally described by Kraepelin (1896/1987), who used a chronic, deteriorating course as the key categorization feature: "The course of dementia praecox [as it was then called] is generally regular and progressive. It is rare to see a substantial remission of the symptoms. . . . The mental impairment remains. . . . The most common outcome in severe forms of dementia praecox is dementia" (pp. 20–21). Because of the perceived unremitting progression of the disorder, Kraepelin wrote of treatment: "After the illness has run its course there is no real possibility of further educational pursuits. . . . It is relatively rare for the patient to be able to return to even a modest degree of mental independence. . . . The treatment of dementia praecox offers few points for intervention" (pp. 21, 24). It is also important to point out that Kraepelin, and many subsequent theorists, viewed the disorder as having an as-yet-undiscovered organic etiology. This belief set the stage for embracing later pharmacologic interventions as cures.

Bleuler (1911/1980) renamed Kraepelin's dementia praecox as schizophrenia and delineated four subtypes according to predominant symptoms. Bleuler was slightly more optimistic about treatment and prognosis for some of the subtypes, but emphasized that the overall prognosis for schizophrenia was grim. If patients returned to a more normal level of functioning, he reasoned, then by definition they probably did not have schizophrenia. The diagnosis, therefore, became associated with a hopeless prognosis, similar to a terminal illness.

When writing of suicidal ideation in these patients, Bleuler went so far as to say:

> People are being forced to continue to live a life that has become unbearable for them for valid reasons . . . it is even worse, when life is made increasingly intolerable for these patients by using every means to subject them to constant humiliating surveillance. Most of our worst restraining measures would be unnecessary, if we were not duty-bound to preserve the patients' lives which, for them, as well as for others, are only of negative value. (1911/1980; pp. 488–489)

Differing nosologies of schizophrenia contributed to the shifts in attitudes toward care in another way. The delineation of the three major types of schizophrenia by Kraepelin, and the addition of the fourth, simple schizophrenia, by Bleuler, were the last nosologic work to achieve wide acceptance until the research and clinical criteria that emerged in the 1970s (e.g., research and diagnostic criteria [RDC], World Health Organization [WHO], International Classification of Diseases [ICD; World Health Organization 1978], Diagnostic and Statistical Manual [DSM; American Psychiatric Association 1952]). Between the turn of the century and the 1960s, research in the field was severely hampered by the absence of any agreement on syndrome definition. This prevented cross-study comparisons or generalization of results from research reports. The absence of methodologically solid research, largely due to poor diagnostic definitions, cast a deeper shadow of hopelessness about the disorder.

In addition to nosologic issues, the structure of the mental health care system itself intensified the sense of pessimism about schizophrenia. During the first half of this century, care of most types of psychiatric disorders was predominantly palliative rather than curative and took place in institutional settings. Indeed, the state hospital was the cornerstone upon which modern psychiatry was built (Grob 1987). By the mid-1950s, nearly 50% of all psychiatric care occurred in state hospitals (Sharfstein 1984); 45% of state hospital patients had been residents for over 10 years (Yolles 1977). For the individual with schizophrenia, who was seen as having a chronic, deteriorating course, the best that could be offered was often lifetime institutionalization. In patients who were warehoused, frequently in overcrowded, nonstimulating environments, some features of the disorder were actually exacerbated by the institutional syndrome of apathy, withdrawal, and infantile behavior (Paul and Lentz 1977).

Until the late 1950s, therefore, the diagnosis of schizophrenia remained tantamount to a medical diagnosis of cancer. Several forces shaped more optimism about this diagnosis from the late 1950s to the mid-1970s. The first was the introduction of successful pharmacologic interventions in schizophrenia. Although medications had been tried for years (Bleuler describes the moderate usefulness of atropine and apomorphine [1911/1978]), no medication before chlorpromazine had produced such a dramatic suppression of acute psychotic symptoms. The discovery of chlorpromazine was followed by the rapid development and widespread use of many more neuroleptic medications. Acute symptom suppression became viewed as the treatment of choice, somehow controlling the assumed, but unknown, organic lesion.

Concurrent with pharmacologic advances, rumblings of change were heard in the mental health care delivery system. These changes were partially fueled by the fantasy of pharmacologic cures, but were also fed by a growing awareness of poor conditions in state hospitals. Attention to the conditions of the chronic psychiatric patient was part of the larger political scene in the United States that reached new heights of social consciousness in the 1960s. Freedom and civil liberties became issues of daily, vital importance and were ultimately extended to institutionalized psychiatric patients. Szasz (1976) and Laing (1967) at this point even construed schizophrenia as a diagnosis created for social control of aberrant behavior, rather than a syndrome based on empirical evidence.

These forces culminated in the community mental health center (CMHC) movement, embodied in the 1963 Community Mental Health

Centers Act. This act led to a massive shift of psychiatric care from the inpatient, institutional setting to an outpatient, community-based model. The goals of the "deinstitutionalization" movement (Mechanic 1987) were noble, although shortsighted: to reintegrate the chronic psychiatric patient into the community. This would have a therapeutic effect by eliminating the isolation of the institution and allowing these patients to experience the gratifications of normal life in a protected manner. The system would work not only by restoring freedom, but also (through the use of medications) by controlling symptoms to the point where individuals with schizophrenia could function nearly normally.

The effects of the Community Mental Health Centers Act were dramatic: by 1977, only 9% of psychiatric care was provided by state hospitals (Sharfstein 1984). Unfortunately, the longer term effects have included grave consequences for the chronically mentally ill, including those with schizophrenia. Although state hospitals have decreased their occupancies, the use of psychiatric beds at nonstate hospitals has dramatically increased (Goldman et al. 1983). State hospitals may have lowered the average length of stay, but the absolute number of admissions, occurring in a "revolving door" pattern, has increased. Data suggest that people with schizophrenia alone may account for 500,000 admissions per year (Goldman 1984).

When we look into the community, the status of people with schizophrenia is in some ways worse than during the institutional era (Lehman 1983). As a group, most chronically mentally ill people are unable to manage daily living, are poorly fed and housed, and receive inadequate medical care (Goldstrom and Manderscheid 1981). The transition to community care was neither adequately planned nor adequately financed to replace the long-term institutions or to function as a total care system for those who are chronically mentally ill (Group for the Advancement of Psychiatry 1982, 1983).

The naive hope was that medications would create a group of patients who needed no more than medication management, transitional support, and perhaps supportive psychotherapy—not the full range of psychiatric, social, and medical care. However, medications have not been as effective as had been originally anticipated: up to one-half of individuals with schizophrenia may not benefit from current medications (Gardos and Cole 1976). Those that do may have as high as a 50% 2-year relapse rate if medication is the only treatment used (Hogarty et al. 1979). Many people with schizophrenia do not take medications, even if they prove effective, because the side effects are so intolerable (Drake and Erlich 1985; Van Putten and May 1978).

By the early 1980s, therefore, it became clear that schizophrenia had not been cured, and indeed, that patients might be worse off in some ways than before. A new wave of pessimism replaced the almost euphoric optimism of the 1960s and early 1970s. An additional complication has been the general upheaval about health care policy and financing in this country. There has been increasing reluctance on the part of reimbursement parties, private or federal, to care for chronic illness in general, let alone chronic psychiatric illness such as schizophrenia.

The pessimism has been tempered some by the discovery of brain imaging techniques in the late 1970s with the renewed hope of finding the ever-elusive etiology of the disorder. It has also been tempered by the patient advocacy movement, which is determined not to let these patients be forgotten once more in the community counterparts of the back wards of state hospitals. But there is still a sense of futility: total institutionalization clearly does not work, but if suppression of symptoms is not curative, then how can the patient with schizophrenia be helped? In the last few years, data on the longitudinal course of schizophrenia have emerged, both in the United States and internationally, that suggest courses of action in managing this disorder.

Longitudinal Studies of Schizophrenia

The data summarized here are drawn from two issues of *Schizophrenia Bulletin* (Goldstein and Tsuang 1990a; McGlashan and Carpenter 1988). The first issue was devoted to a comprehensive review of all the longitudinal studies on the disorder, and the second synthesized the data available on gender differences in schizophrenia.

In these issues of the journal, some clinical beliefs were confirmed, but others were refuted. McGlashan (1988) reviewed the North American longitudinal studies of schizophrenia and found that the 30- to 40-year outcome for about half of these patients is much better than expected or predicted from their short-term (less than 5 years) outcome. He summarized what has been learned about the long-term outcome of schizophrenia:

1. Schizophrenia is a chronic, disabling illness.
2. There is an increased risk of suicide, physical illness, and early death in individuals with schizophrenia. Suicide rates vary from 5% to 10% in this population, and longevity is decreased by up to 10 years in comparison with the general population.
3. Although it is chronic and disabling, schizophrenia does not ultimately lead to permanent, irreversible deterioration. The "raging brainstorms" of the first 5 to 10 years seem more often than not to die down to a more stable residual stage.

4. The course of schizophrenia is heterogeneous. Although methodological differences between samples may confuse this picture, the trend toward different courses and outcomes seems clear.
5. It is important to investigate the differences in the samples studied. This exercise may enable us to unearth some aspects of successful treatment and management that have nothing to do with more acute medical approaches to these patients.
6. We do not have any evidence at this time to indicate that our current treatment strategies significantly alter the long-term course of the illness.
7. Sociocultural forces (e.g., industrialization) appear to be important factors in eventual outcome.
8. There are gender differences in both course and outcome.
9. Psychiatric comorbidity may play an important role in outcome; for example, there may be a poorer prognosis for those with coexisting substance abuse.
10. Clinical outcome should be viewed as part of a multidimensional process, not as a conclusive description of one point in time.

One of the most important findings is that the course of schizophrenia is not uniform. Angst (1988) summarized Ciompi's (1980) data, which suggest a number of different pathways that the illness can take. Symptoms can be acute or chronic at onset, and the course can be quite varied, with both poor and good long-term outcomes. Of particular interest was the finding that good outcome was associated with two pathways: an undulating course characterized by recurrent bouts of psychosis, or an initial episode or two of psychosis with a gradual but steady reduction in symptoms over a longer period of time.

Harding (1988) analyzed data from the Vermont Longitudinal Research Project (VLRP) (Harding et al. 1987) and the Burgholzi Hospital Study (Bleuler 1911/1978), applying Ciompi's pathways. She then compared the proportions of each of the three data sets that followed each path. The rates of recovery of those with mild remaining symptomatology in all studies ranged from 50% to 62% (VLRP). The proportions of the specific samples that took each pathway were different. The majority of the "good outcome" group from Ciompi's (1980) study and from the Burgholzi sample had an acute onset with an undulating course, whereas the majority of the "good outcome" group in the Vermont sample had a chronic onset followed by an undulating course. Methodological differences may explain these cross-study variations.

Cross-cultural comparisons of Western and non-Western courses of schizophrenia also reveal some interesting findings. Lin and Kleinman

(1988) reviewed studies conducted elsewhere than in the United States, Canada, and Europe and reported that these studies indicate a much higher rate of total remission (up to 65%) than the Western studies do. Questions regarding diagnostic comparability are obviously important, but these findings are similar to those reported in the International Pilot Study of Schizophrenia (Sartorius et al. 1986), in which standardized entry criteria were used in all countries and follow-up was consistent across sites. Follow-up at 2 years was significantly better for patients in the developing countries than in the industrialized ones (Sartorius et al. 1986). Some methodological issues have been raised, however, regarding the true diagnoses of those patients with good outcomes.

Even if we allow for methodological problems within and between studies, it is clear that schizophrenia is not always associated with poor outcome. Furthermore, it appears that even in those individuals with a poorer outcome, the schizophrenic process is not relentlessly progressive but may plateau after 5 to 10 years of manifest illness, leaving people with chronic disability but not continuing waves of deepening psychosis. These two findings are vital to understanding what will be helpful in the care and treatment of people with this disorder.

An essential issue in designing a comprehensive approach to these patients is to determine what (if any) baseline features, interventions, or life experiences differentiate those with good outcomes from those with poor outcomes. We are referring here to *long-term* positive adjustment; obviously, if the disorder is at its worst in the 5 to 10 years after onset and if outcome is measured or determined by rehospitalization or a recurrence of symptoms within a 5- to 10-year follow-up period, then most of the people with eventual good outcomes will be missed.

Interstudy differences in the definition of "outcome" make this a difficult but not impossible question to answer. Reviews of the long-term studies (Angst 1988; Lin and Kleinman 1988; McGlashan 1988) suggest that outcome after 20 years is related to premorbid functioning, gender, marital status, and socioeconomic status at baseline. It is important to note that the content and severity of initial presentation and the response to medications—classic predictors of a good prognosis in an acute care model—are not useful in predicting long-term outcome in patients with schizophrenia. In fact, the long-term studies have demonstrated neither the clear efficacy of one treatment over another nor the relationship of the different types of acute treatment to outcome.

Gender differences in schizophrenia have been recognized since 1919, when Kraepelin labeled dementia praecox as a disorder of young males. Differences have been described in age of onset, premorbid functioning, outcome, and brain abnormalities (Goldstein and Tsuang 1990b). There is evidence that the prognosis for long-term outcome may be better for women. Whether this is due to biological differences, such as hormonal or brain abnormalities, or sociocultural differences in role definition is unclear. It *is* clear that the investigation of these possible relationships is complex and requires a longitudinal perspective rather than one that focused either on acute treatment of symptoms or on a fixed-deficit model.

The Comprehensive Approach

It is clear that the time has come to look at the treatment of schizophrenia from a multidimensional, comprehensive longitudinal perspective. This approach incorporates the merits of other approaches (acute and chronic care models) but recognizes a greater potential for healing and growth in individuals with schizophrenia than has characterized previous approaches. This perspective should address the adult developmental issues of men and women with schizophrenia, as well as take into account the biological etiologies and symptomatic treatments. To be successful, such a perspective requires a rehabilitative focus, with attention paid to the vocational and social aspects of the disorder. In this book, we address each of these dimensions of the comprehensive approach and describe its policy implications as well.

This volume is intended for both medical and nonmedical staff working with individuals with schizophrenia in a variety of settings. Policymakers at the state and federal levels will also find it helpful, and it should be of great interest to patient advocacy groups, to families of people with schizophrenia, and to those with schizophrenia themselves. We believe that it is time to ask new questions, to place in a new framework the information that comes from our patients and their families, and to broaden our perspective to incorporate the diversity of pathways that this illness can take through an individual's lifetime.

References

American Psychiatric Association: Diagnostic and Statistical Manual: Mental Disorders. Washington, DC, American Psychiatric Association, 1952

Angst J: European long-term follow-up studies of schizophrenia. Schizophr Bull 14(4):501–513, 1988

Bleuler E: The Schizophrenic Disorders: The Long-Term Patient and Family Studies (1911). Translated by Clemens SM. New Haven, CT, Yale University Press, 1978

Bleuler E: Dementia Praecox or The Group of Schizophrenias (1911). Translated by Zinkin J. New York, International Universities Press, 1980

Ciompi L: Catamnestic long-term study on the course of life and aging of schizophrenics. Schizophr Bull 6:606-618, 1980

Drake RE, Ehrlich J: Suicide attempts associated with akathisia. Am J Psychiatry 142:499–501, 1985

Gardos G, Cole JO: Maintenance antipsychotic therapy: is the cure worse than the disease? Am J Psychiatry 133:32–36, 1976

Goldman HH: Epidemiology, in The Chronic Mental Patient: Five Years Later. Edited by Talbott JA. Orlando, FL, Grune & Stratton, 1984

Goldman HH, Adams NH, Taube CA: Deinstitutionalization: the data demythologized. Hosp Community Psychiatry 34:129–134, 1983

Goldstein JM, Tsuang MT (eds): Schizophr Bull 16(2), 1990a (whole issue)

Goldstein JM, Tsuang MT: Gender and schizophrenia: an introduction and synthesis of findings. Schizophr Bull 16(2):179–183, 1990b

Goldstrom ID, Manderscheid RW: The chronically mentally ill: a descriptive analysis from the uniform client data instrument. Community Support Service Journal 2:4–9, 1981

Grob G: The forging of mental health policy in America: World War II to new frontier. J Hist Med Allied Sci 42:410–446, 1987

Group for the Advancement of Psychiatry: The Positive Aspects of Long Term Hospitalization in the Public Sector for Chronic Psychiatric Patients. New York, Brunner/Mazel, 1982

Group for the Advancement of Psychiatry: Community Psychiatry: A Reappraisal. New York, Brunner/Mazel, 1983

Harding CM: Course types in schizophrenia: an analysis of European and American studies. Schizophr Bull 14(4):633–643, 1988

Harding CM, Brooks GW, Ashikega T, et al: The Vermont longitudinal study of persons with severe mental illness, I: methodology, study sample and overall status 32 years later. Am J Psychiatry 144:718–726, 1987

Hogarty GE, Schooler NR, Ulrich R, et al: Fluphenazine and social therapy in the aftercare of schizophrenic patients. Arch Gen Psychiatry 36:1283–1294, 1979

Kraepelin E: Dementia praecox (1896), in The Clinical Roots of the Schizophrenia Concept. Translated and edited by Cutting J, Shepard M. New York, Cambridge University Press, 1987

Laing RD: The Politics of Experience. Middlesex, England, Penguin, 1967, pp 84–107

Lehman A: The well-being of chronic mental patients. Arch Gen Psychiatry 40:369–373, 1983

Lin KM, Kleinman AM: Psychopathology and clinical course of schizophrenia: a cross-cultural perspective. Schizophr Bull 14(4):555–567, 1988

McGlashan TH: A selective review of recent North American long-term follow-up studies of schizophrenia. Schizophr Bull 14(4):515–542, 1988

McGlashan TH, Carpenter TW (eds): Schizophr Bull 14(4), 1988 (whole issue)

Mechanic D: Correcting misperceptions in mental health policy: strategies for improved care of the seriously mentally ill. Milbank Q 65:203–230, 1987

Paul GL, Lentz RJ: Psychosocial Treatment of Chronic Mental Patients: Milieu Versus Social-Learning Programs. Cambridge, MA, Harvard University Press, 1977

Sartorius N, Jablensky A, Korten A, et al: early manifestations and first-contact incidence of schizophrenia in different cultures. Psychol Med 16:909–928, 1986

Sharfstein SS: Sociopolitical issues affecting patients with chronic schizophrenia, in Schizophrenia: Treatment, Management, and Rehabilitation. Edited by Bellack AS. Orlando, FL, Grune & Stratton, 1984

Szasz TS: Schizophrenia: The Sacred Symbol of Psychiatry. New York, Basic Books, 1976

Van Putten T, May PRA: Akinetic depression in schizophrenia. Arch Gen Psychiatry 35:1101–1107, 1978

World Health Organization: Mental Disorders: Glossary and Guide to Their Classification in Accordance With the Ninth Revision of the International Classification of Diseases. Geneva, World Health Organization, 1978

Yolles SF: A critical appraisal of community health services, in New Trends of Psychiatry in the Community. Edited by Serban G, Astrachan BA. Cambridge, MA, Ballinger, 1977

2

The Adult Developmental Perspective and Its Implications for Schizophrenia

Adulthood constitutes the bulk of a person's life, spanning many years and experiences. Although a debilitating illness such as schizophrenia exerts profound effects on a person's life, the illness alone hardly defines the person over the course of adulthood. An adult developmental perspective may aid in understanding the experience of having schizophrenia and guide interventions to help people adapt to this illness and enhance the quality of their lives.

In this chapter, we explore some of the implications of an adult developmental perspective on schizophrenia. Such a discussion is, of necessity, speculative because it attempts to integrate two areas of study—the long-term course of schizophrenia and normal adult development (Levinson 1986; McGlashan and Carpenter 1988; Neugarten 1979)—that are themselves in their infancy. Key points in the longitudinal studies of schizophrenia and key concepts of normal adult development are summarized and then integrated into speculations about the adult developmental experiences of people with this disorder. These speculations in turn have implications for further research and for treatment.

The Long-Term Course of Schizophrenia

Although the outcomes of schizophrenia are quite varied, it is, in general, a severely disabling syndrome, and its outcomes are typically worse than those of other major mental disorders. Schizophrenia's typical course appears to be one of deterioration of functioning during the first decade of the illness with a subsequent plateau or even modest improvement later in life. It is associated with increased risk of suicide, particularly among younger patients, and increased morbidity and mortality because of a variety of physical illnesses later in life. These factors result in an overall reduction in life expectancy of about 10 years compared to the general population. There is also evidence that outcomes may be worse for men than for women and that there are different, relatively independent dimensions of outcome such as symptoms, social function, and work (McGlashan 1988).

Caveats about the variability of outcome aside, a typical picture of the course of schizophrenia is as follows: it begins in adolescence or early adulthood, interferes significantly with development during these years, and leaves the affected person with various deficits in the capacities to work, form interpersonal relations, and function independently. People with chronic schizophrenia typically are unable to work or are underemployed, are unmarried, and are dependent on their families or on caretakers for shelter and basic support. In order to simplify this discussion, we will use this prototype as a reference point to illustrate the application of adult developmental concepts to schizophrenia. Obviously this approach only begins to explore the great variability and complexity of adult life experiences of people with this syndrome.

Normal Adult Development

Central to current theories about normal adult development is the concept that an adult's life has a structure that evolves in fairly predictable ways over the years (Levinson 1986). The stages of adult development can be characterized according to a sequence of fundamental tasks. The boundaries between stages are punctuated by critical transitions that are characterized by reappraisal, a search for new possibilities, and modifications to one's life structure in preparation for the next stage (Levinson 1986). This structural view of adult life, as studied in men, has been criticized for overlooking considerable fluidity in the timing and progression of these adult tasks—a fluidity that seems particularly evident in recent times of major social change (Neugarten 1979). In essence, the stages of adult development have become less age-bound.

Despite the validity of this criticism, the attempt to make sense out of the progression of experiences over the adult years remains valuable. At the very least, there is a strong cultural belief that adult life proceeds according to some basic agenda (Levinson et al. 1978; Sheehy 1976; Vaillant 1977). It is reasonable to assume that these prevailing beliefs determine how members of a culture perceive and evaluate the lives of people with schizophrenia and that these beliefs even influence the patients' perceptions of themselves. Outcome research and psychiatric treatments take an implicitly normative view of life, which should take into account an adult developmental perspective.

Among a variety of similar formulations of normal adult development, Levinson's (Levinson 1986; Levinson et al. 1978) serves as a useful model. He divides adult development into three main stages: early adulthood (ages 17 to 45), middle adulthood (ages 40 to 65), and late adulthood (age 60 and beyond). Levinson also identifies three critical transitions that account for the overlap in these age categories: the early adult transition (ages 17 to 22), the midlife transition (ages 40 to 45), and the late adult transition (ages 60 to 65).

The early adult transition is a time of individuation and realignment of relationships with one's parental family. A person begins to assert "adulthood" and to establish a plan for the early adult years. The entire early adult stage—ages 17 to 45—is one of great energy, passion, and ambition. The major tasks of this stage include forming and pursuing aspirations, creating a niche in society, establishing and raising a family, and pursuing a career. It is a time of major achievements and goal attainment—a time when independence and self-sufficiency are most valued. Because of this dynamism, early adulthood is also a period of great risk and stress because of increasing demands and the sense of urgency attached to the achievement of major goals. It can therefore be a time of crushing blows to one's self-esteem.

At the midlife transition, one takes stock of the early adult years; "what if" fantasies are common. Questions are raised about the life structure established thus far, and new goals may be established for middle adulthood. This reassessment and realignment can produce considerable disruption in a person's life, commonly referred to as the "midlife crisis."

Successful negotiation of this midlife transition can set the stage for a middle adulthood characterized by an increased capacity to nurture others, a more compassionate, judicious, and reflective view of life, and less buffeting by inner conflicts and external demands. There can be a coming to terms with oneself (both strengths and shortcomings), and a sense of attainment and accommodation. In his or her various roles, the person feels a sense of experience and of satisfaction in conveying this experience to others. One may set about to accomplish important goals in the time that remains. The person also becomes increasingly aware of issues of mortality. On the other hand, an unsatisfactory resolution of the midlife transition can lead to depression, demoralization, and a great sense of loss.

In the late life transition, one begins to adjust to late adulthood; this is again a time of reappraisal and realignment. The person begins to anticipate losses and prepares for major role transitions. Late adult life is, on the one hand, characterized by many losses of work, friends, family members, and roles. A decline in physical health and the issue of one's own mortality loom large. However, this can also be a time for new roles and activities: grandparenting, retirement careers, expanded leisure, and serving as a wise adviser. Late adulthood can be a time of great life satisfaction (Campbell et al. 1976).

It is worthwhile to note that "quality-of-life" researchers have explored the influence of adult development on well-being. Satisfaction with life seems to increase with age, although younger people express more transient happiness and excitement about life (Diener 1984). Not surprisingly, the unmarried and unemployed are less satisfied with their lives than are those with stable marriages and jobs (Andrews and Withey 1976; Campbell et al. 1976). There may be some interaction between gender and age on life satisfaction. Life satisfaction for men may increase with age, whereas it appears to remain constant for women; hence, younger women express more happiness than do younger men, but this pattern is reversed among the elderly (Medley 1980; Spreitzer and Snyder 1974).

Schizophrenia and Adult Development

What are the implications of these two bodies of data and theory in formulating notions about adult development in people with schizophrenia? The following speculations are organized around Levinson's stages of adulthood (1986; Levinson et al. 1978).

Early Adulthood

What is perhaps most striking about the course of schizophrenia is that the most virulent phase of this disorder coincides with that high-energy stage of adulthood characterized by the greatest pressures for self-definition, independence, and achievement. The often tumultuous problems of the so-called young adult chronic patients (Pepper and Ryglewicz 1984; Sheets et al. 1982) are readily understood in terms of the collision of normal youthful aspirations, passions, and social pressures with the progressive barriers to meeting life's demands that are raised by schizophrenia. According to the long-term studies, the young adult afflicted with schizophrenia faces a decade of progressive loss of function or failure to achieve functions just when peers are experiencing their years of most rapid growth into adult roles. Failures at school, work, and in interpersonal relationships devastate self-esteem and sense of identity, contribute to a profound sense of alienation from family and friends, and undoubtedly account at least in part for the high rate of suicide among these people (Pepper and Ryglewicz 1984).

The major tasks of this stage of life—work, marriage, parenthood—are largely aborted. In a sense, the young adult with schizophrenia is locked into the early adult transition—unable to gain independence from parents, unable to be self-sufficient, unable to establish a life agenda to carry through early adulthood, and often left with no choice but to arrive at a self-identity focused on patienthood. At a time when peers are forming new alliances with co-workers, friends, and spouses, the social network of the young adult with schizophrenia revolves more and more around other people with mental illness and service providers.

A variety of developmental considerations must be taken into account in planning treatment for these young adults. First, this is the time of greatest risk to the patient's physical safety. In response to the frustrations of failure to succeed in normal life tasks, the young adult with schizophrenia is likely to engage in various self-destructive behaviors, including suicide, substance abuse, and recklessness. Normal levels of adult activity may be replaced by a daily pattern marked by inactivity, lack of exercise, smoking, poor diet, and poor self-care, all of which may contribute to the higher lifetime morbidity of schizophrenia. Second, the failure to achieve adequate self-identity (often with increased dependency on the family of origin) results in a variety of psychological difficulties, including excessive anxiety about sexual orientation, frantic shifts from one life plan to another, geographic transiency, and difficulties in establishing relationships with others. Third, the marked discrepancy between aspirations and actual achievement leads to demoralization and rage, which interfere with the patient's ability to work toward realistic treatment goals. This pattern contributes to the often realistic perception of these patients as resistant to or rejecting of treatment (Pepper and Ryglewicz 1984).

To work with these patients in the face of such bitter realities, clinicians and other care providers will find an adult developmental perspective extremely helpful. Knowing that the illness is likely to become less virulent with age at least permits patients, families, and service providers to feel some hope. It can be difficult for patients to accept hope at this stage of life because it requires a major readjustment of expectations downward, a task that most of us do not have to face until much later in life. Therefore, support and safety may be the hallmarks of treatment goals at this stage. After age 30, patients may be better able to deal with lowered expectations and hence to become more amenable to rehabilitation efforts and psychotherapy aimed at enhancing self-esteem and setting realistic life goals. This process might be seen as a premature midlife transition.

Middle Adulthood

Very little is known about the lives of people with schizophrenia beyond young adulthood. Successful realignment of expectations may account for the decrease in adverse outcomes and improvement in life satisfaction seen around midlife in these patients (Lehman et al., in press).

It is at this middle stage of adulthood that psychotherapy aimed at providing patients with a realistic perspective on their lives, both on what they have been through and on what they can expect in the future, may be most helpful. In many ways, this transition is the same as for anyone at midlife—that is, patients must take stock of their lives and of their fulfilled and unfulfilled dreams, arrive at some accommodation to the realities of life thus far, and make plans for the next couple of decades. Fortunately, the long-term studies suggest that the illness has largely run its course by this time. Therefore, patients will experience fewer unexpected losses and failures and may now be able to establish a better sense of themselves. The major risk is total demoralization and resignation to a life of unhappiness. In the best scenario, the patient will be able to accept more realistic expectations, will actually achieve gainful, though limited, employment, and will establish a stable social support network independent of parents and care providers. The middle-aged patient may also have much advice to offer younger patients. Mutual benefits could result from such nurturing interactions.

It is unclear to what extent the "burnout" seen in so many middle-aged people with schizophrenia reflects the natural biological course of this illness and to what extent it represents a demoralized resolution to the process of taking stock. Thus, midlife may be a time to try more rather than less with these patients.

Older Adulthood

The most important point to make about normal development in older adulthood is that it is the time at which, for most people, loss becomes a central experience of life. In some ways, the person with schizophrenia has less to lose. The patient's life begins at this stage to have more possibilities in common with the lives of his or her contemporaries: no job, no spouse, living alone, declining physical health. Does this mean that the person with schizophrenia can feel more comfortable with others at this age? We do not know. Indeed, extremely little is known about elderly people with schizophrenia living in the community.

The limited literature suggests that both the positive psychotic symptoms (delusions, hallucinations, and disordered thinking) and negative symptoms of schizophrenia diminish after midlife (Cohler and Ferrono 1987). The relative contributions to this improvement of biological and psychological maturation and of changing social expectations remain unknown. In a discussion of older adults in California board-and-care homes, Lamb (1987) states,

> Many patients reach an adjustment similar to successful retirement—they spend their time reading, puttering about, and interacting with their families. . . . Maturation also seems a factor, since age makes a person less impulsive and more philosophical in the face of adversity and disappointment. (p. 201)

But Lamb goes on to warn that decompensation later in life may follow the losses of loved ones and social supports that accompany aging.

Gender Differences

Gender differences in the course of schizophrenia have their own implications for an adult developmental perspective on this disorder. Such gender differences have been found in the areas of premorbid history, symptomatology, brain morphology, brain functioning, neurochemistry, family transmission, course, and treatment response (Goldstein and Tsuang 1990). Young men with schizophrenia appear to be at greater risk for adverse outcomes than are young women with schizophrenia (Leventhal et al. 1984). This may be due to differences in the earlier age of onset of the illness among men (Loranger 1984), to gender-related differences in role opportunities and expectations (e.g., that women are more likely to marry and have children, thus establishing some normative role functioning), or to other gender-related biological and psychological differences in adjustment during young adulthood (Torrey 1989; Weinberger 1987).

Gender differences have also been found in quality-of-life experiences among people with chronic mental illnesses, predominantly schizophrenia, across the stages of adult development (Lehman et al., in press). In terms of functional status and resources, chronically mentally ill men reported more financial resources, but women who were chronically mentally ill engaged in more social relationships across the life cycle. Life satisfaction for these women increased with age, whereas the men's satisfaction with various aspects of their lives either decreased or remained the same. A midlife transition that differs between men and women with severe mental illnesses, perhaps related to gender differences in work and parenting roles, may account for these differences in life satisfaction.

With regard to women with schizophrenia, the treatment tasks may need to be broadened. In the past, most women married and could depend on husbands to care for them while they were mentally ill; this may explain some of the better outcomes for women. This support was even more assured if children were involved. Today, a young woman with schizophrenia is not only likely to be unmarried but is also likely to be a parent. The woman with schizophrenia is much less likely to avoid this normal role of parenthood than the man (Seeman 1986). As a result, treatment from an adult developmental perspective must not only protect the woman from substance abuse, suicide, and recklessness but must also consider protecting her from unwanted pregnancies and treating both herself and her children, if she already has them, as a dyadic unit. The latter task involves educating these women in basic parenting skills and providing multiple levels of social support (housing, homemaking, and child care). Treatment should be sensitive to the implications of parenthood as a relatively common developmental event among women with schizophrenia.

It is important to stress that there is evidence that women with schizophrenia may not be as likely to plateau as men are. They may require more medication and may have renewed symptomatic episodes with menopause. Such episodes may actually be worse in childless women, because this is the stage in a woman's life when she must face the termination of one aspect of her feminine identity. If a woman has not had any children or has lost her children because of her mental illness, the despair may be severe (Salokongas 1983; Seeman 1986).

In brief, the generally later age of onset and better earlier course among women with schizophrenia compared to men with the disorder have major developmental implications. Whereas men with schizophrenia must struggle with preadult and early adult transition arrests in development (such as the failure to complete high school or to move out of the parental home), women typically must deal with problems (such as parenthood) that are associated with a later developmental stage.

Conclusions and Recommendations

Our current knowledge about normal adult development and the long-term course of schizophrenia lead to the following treatment and research agenda:

1. A long-term perspective on schizophrenia requires a shift away from the current emphasis on the acute, crisis phases of the disorder and a move toward consideration of adult developmental issues over the course of the patient's lifetime. Thus, the adult developmental perspective demands a concern with outcomes beyond symptom suppression. This means that, in addition to the ongoing attention paid to young adults with schizophrenia, researchers need to look at the more quiescent years of the disorder—those of late young adulthood, midlife, and late adulthood. We need to ask what happens biologically, psychologically, and socially to these patients after age 30.
2. More must be learned about the efficacy of different modes of therapy and rehabilitation at the different stages of life. Can we identify "critical" transition points in the course of the illness and of the patient's adjustment to them? If so, do these transition points offer any guidance for the timing of interventions? Is it best to do more for younger than for older patients, or should we actually try to do more with patients later in life?
3. More data are needed on the natural developmental course (or, at least the course under usual treatment) of the various dimensions of outcome (neurocognitive, symptoms, interpersonal relations, psychological adaptation, work, and so on) in schizophrenia. These data can then establish a baseline against which to assess the efficacy of various interventions.
4. Significant differences appear to exist between the life experiences of men and women with schizophrenia. More research must be conducted to enable us to understand these gender differences and to account for them in the provision of services.
5. Finally, we need to examine how to incorporate an understanding of adult developmental issues into the treatment and rehabilitation of people with schizophrenia. Such incorporation is one of the best ways to ensure that the services we provide are appropriately individualized and that we view these people not only in the context of their illness but also in relationship to normal adult development.

References

Andrews FM, Withey SB: Social Indicators of Well-Being: America's Perception of Quality of Life. New York, Plenum, 1976

Campbell A, Converse PE, Rodgers WL: The Quality of American Life. New York, Russell Sage Foundation, 1976

Cohler BJ, Ferrono CL: Schizophrenia and the adult lifecourse, in Schizophrenia and Aging. Edited by Miller NE, Cohen GD. New York, Guilford, 1987

Diener E: Subjective well-being. Psychol Bull 95:542–575, 1984

Goldstein JD, Tsuang MT: Gender and schizophrenia: an introduction and synthesis of findings. Schizophr Bull 16(2):179–183, 1990

Lamb HR: Predisposition to schizophrenia: Breakdown or adaptation in later life, in Schizophrenia and Aging. Edited by Miller NE, Cohen GD. New York, Guilford, 1987

Lehman AF, Slaughter JG, Myers CP: Quality-of-life experiences of the chronically mentally ill: gender and stages of life effects. Evaluation and Program Planning (in press)

Leventhal DB, Schuck JR, Rothstein H: Gender differences in schizophrenia. J Nerv Ment Dis 172:464–467, 1984

Levinson DJ: A conception of adult development. Am Psychol 41:3–13, 1986

Levinson DJ, Darrow CN, Klein EB, et al: Seasons of a Man's Life. New York, Knopf, 1978

Loranger AW: Sex difference in age of onset of schizophrenia. Arch Gen Psychiatry 41:157–161, 1984

McGlashan TH: A selective review of recent North American long-term follow-up studies of schizophrenia. Schizophr Bull 14(4):515–542, 1988

McGlashan TH, Carpenter WT: Long-term follow-up studies of schizophrenia. Schizophr Bull 14(4):497–500, 1988

Medley ML: Life satisfaction across the four stages of adult life. Int J Aging Hum Dev 11:193–209, 1980

Neugarten BL: Time, age, and the life cycle. Am J Psychiatry 136:887–894, 1979

Pepper B, Ryglewicz H (eds): Advances in Treating the Young Adult Chronic Patient (New Directions in Mental Health Services, no. 21). San Francisco, Jossey-Bass, 1984

Salokongas K: Prognostic implications of the sex of schizophrenic patients. Br J Psychiatry 142:145–151, 1983

Seeman MV: Current outcome in schizophrenia: women versus men. Acta Psychiatr Scand 73:609–617, 1986

Sheehy G: Passages: Predictable Crises of Adult Life. New York, Dutton, 1976

Sheets JL, Prevost JA, Reihman J: Young adult chronic patients: three hypothesized subgroups. Hosp Community Psychiatry 33:197–203, 1982

Spreitzer E, Snyder EE: Correlates of life satisfaction among the aged. J Gerontol 29:454–458, 1974

Torrey EF: The epidemiology of schizophrenia: questions needing answers, in Schizophrenia: Scientific Progress. Edited by Schulz SC, Tamminga CA. New York, Oxford University Press, 1989

Vaillant G: Adaptation to Life. Boston, MA, Little, Brown, 1977

Weinberger DR: Implications of normal brain development for the pathogenesis of schizophrenia. Arch Gen Psychiatry 44:660–669, 1987

3

The Postinstitutional Generation: Cohort Effects and Long-Term Outcome in Schizophrenia

In this chapter, we will review some of the factors that have affected people who developed schizophrenia during the years since "deinstitutionalization" began to be implemented. We will highlight the inadequacies of the current treatment system, the adverse effects of abuse of alcohol and other drugs, and the dangers of homelessness. We will also raise the question whether the long-term outcomes of the current generation of people with schizophrenia differ substantially from previous cohorts.

Cohort Effects

Much of the variability in outcome among people with schizophrenia may be due to the historical and sociocultural dimensions of their lives. These differences are often called cohort effects. A cohort is a group of people who are observed over a period of time to determine the effect of a particular intervention or experience they have shared. A cohort can be defined in a number of ways—for example, by geographic location or by generational time. Thus, a group of people born in the same set of years is called a generation cohort, or an age-specific cohort (Feinstein 1977). Because each generation cohort is exposed to a specific set of secular changes, comparing cohorts from different eras within a sample allows us to study the features of social history that influence development, attitudes, and behaviors.

Attending to age-specific effects in longitudinal research is critical for at least two reasons (Stewart and Healy 1989). First, it increases our understanding of a particular sample and reveals what may be major differences within that sample. For example, Elder (1978; Elder et al. 1985) reanalyzed the Oakland Growth Study data to demonstrate that the age of the children at the time of the Great Depression was a major determinant of its effects on their later lives. Elder (1986) also showed that age was an important factor in understanding the impact of World War II experience on men's subsequent adult lives. Second, cohort effects help to explain the differences or inconsistencies between samples, because some social events, especially those that create unusual or unexpected conditions for the transition to adulthood (such as the experience of war), critically affect the course of later development.

In long-term follow-up studies of people with schizophrenia, age-specific cohort effects may be critical for both reasons. Within-sample differences should be investigated to determine whether important social changes have influenced particular subgroups, and differences between samples should also be examined for the influence of historical factors. A variety of sociocultural changes have potentially affected the younger cohorts of people with schizophrenia (Bachrach 1982; Minkoff 1987). An entire generation of people with schizophrenia has developed the illness, interacted with the mental health system, and entered adulthood during an era in which the locus of treatment has shifted to the community and while other profound sociocultural changes have been occurring. Much of the literature on chronic mental illness during the 1980s, in fact, has assumed that historical changes have defined a cohort of patients who differ substantially from the prior generation of people with chronic mental illness (Caton 1981; Lamb 1982; Pepper et al. 1981).

The Postinstitutional Generation

The confluence of several factors—new medications, changing belief systems, and economic and legal influences—led to a decrease in the patient population of public mental hospitals from nearly 600,000 in 1955 to just over 100,000 in 1985, despite the baby-boom generation's having passed through the age of vulnerability to severe mental illness during this time period (Mechanic and Aiken 1987). For patients with schizophrenia who were hospitalized before this era, "deinstitutionalization" in reality usually involved transfer to other institutions, such as nursing homes (Goldman et al. 1986). For these patients, long-term hospitalization as young adults meant that they adjusted to the difficulties of living with schizophrenia and developed an identity in the relatively protected confines of the hospital (Minkoff 1987).

For people who have become ill with schizophrenia since the 1950s, long-term institutional treatment has been largely unavailable; few have become long-stay patients in psychiatric hospitals (Barber et al. 1988; Richardson et al. 1985). The great majority have encountered the developmental tasks of late adolescence and early adulthood and the stresses of adjusting to severe mental illness without the structure, protection, and clear identity that the mental hospital once provided (Lamb 1982; Minkoff 1987).

At the same time that treatment philosophy was changing, the postwar baby-boom generation moved through the age of vulnerability to schizophrenia. This large group of people who developed severe mental illness in the postinstitutional era was also exposed to a variety of other critical sociocultural changes, such as the increased availability of illicit drugs and the decreased availability of low-cost housing. A raft of articles throughout the 1980s documented the clinical characteristics, treatment challenges, and personal travails of this postinstitutional generation of young people (see, e.g., Bachrach 1982; Caton 1981; Lamb 1982; Pepper et al. 1981).

In the next section, we will review several critical social hazards to illustrate how they might be affecting the long-term course of the disorder in these individuals.

Hazards of the Postinstitutional Era

The Current Treatment System

Community-based service models were intended to provide an alternative to mental hospital treatment—an alternative that was humane and that allowed people with severe mental illness to have their needs met and to develop their potentials without being excluded from the community. The Community Support System model, developed and disseminated by the National Institute of Mental Health (NIMH), prescribes an array of services, more complex and comprehensive than those formerly provided in hospitals, to be coordinated by a mental health agency and fitted for the individual by a case manager (Stroul 1989).

For such a model to work, several forms of support are required: consistent funding, a strong organizational structure, and the provision of a variety of interlocking services. These requirements have rarely been met, and inadequate treatment has been the norm. The majority of chronically ill patients, including individuals with schizophrenia, depend on underfinanced, fragmented, and grossly insufficient services (Mechanic and Aiken 1987). Most states have not been able to provide the range of services that were formerly available in hospitals, let alone the continuity of rehabilitative services that might improve patients' adjustment.

The protective "safety net" of community treatment has gaping holes so numerous and large that many individuals with schizophrenia (perhaps a majority in urban areas) have been lost to the treatment system entirely. Results from the NIMH Epidemiologic Catchment Area (ECA) study showed that, at the three sites studied, 47%–61% of those individuals with a current diagnosis of schizophrenia or schizophreniform disorder had had no mental health services contacts in the previous 6 months (Regier and Burke 1987). This finding contrasts with epidemiological studies 30 years earlier in which the few nonhospitalized people with schizophrenia tended to be in treatment (see, e.g., Leighton et al. 1963). Untreated people with schizophrenia at one ECA site were judged by psychiatric assessment to be severely disabled and in need of treatment (Von Korff et al. 1985). Without treatment, these people often end up disorganized, decompensated, and unable to care for themselves—and in shelters, on the streets, or in jails.

Few longitudinal data exist regarding the process and course of those who are lost to treatment, but it is clear that patients with schizophrenia frequently drop out of outpatient treatment. In the Boston Psychotherapy of Schizophrenia study (Stanton et al. 1984), investigators attempted to follow up the 48 early "clinical dropouts" 2 years after the study began (Katz et al. 1984). The 19 subjects who had continued to receive treatment of various kinds outside of the study had outcomes quite similar to those who had stayed with the original treatment for 2 years, but the remaining 29 subjects who had dropped out of treatment altogether were unstable, disorganized, and paranoid, and at least 5 were already dead.

In summary, the evidence indicates that only a small proportion of individuals with schizophrenia receive comprehensive community treatment; many others receive inadequate, underfunded, fragmented services; and a substantial proportion, half or more in some areas, receive no treatment. There have been few systematic follow-ups of those who are lost to the system, but indirect evidence indicates that they are often found in nontherapeutic settings such as shelters and jails. There is also some evidence that they have severe functional incapacity and a high rate of early mortality. Thus, profound changes in the treatment system are adversely affecting a majority of individuals with schizophrenia and may be adversely influencing their long-term outcomes. Previous studies of long-term outcome, therefore, may be overly optimistic for the current generation of people with schizophrenia.

Alcohol and Drug Use

In the postinstitutional era, many psychotic and prepsychotic people experiment with alcohol and street drugs. Test and others (1985) found, for example, that in their sample of young schizophrenic patients, 96% had used alcohol, 87% marijuana, 60% stimulants, 50% psychedelics, 42% sedatives, and 17% narcotics. With the exception of alcohol, these rates of drug use are much higher than rates for these subjects' age-matched peers (National Institute on Drug Abuse 1987). People with schizophrenia are also much more likely than their peers to develop psychoactive substance use disorders. Indeed, the ECA studies found that people with schizophrenia in the community had greatly increased rates of alcohol and drug use disorders (Boyd et al. 1984; Regier et al. 1990). Recent U.S. studies also find high rates of alcohol use disorders (Drake et al. 1990) and other drug use disorders (Schneier and Siris 1987) among treated schizophrenic patients.

Comorbid alcohol and drug use disorders have been associated with poor adjustment and poor treatment outcomes. Alcohol, the most commonly abused drug among individuals with schizophrenia, has been associated with a higher incidence of the following:

- Delusions (Barbee et al. 1989);
- Hallucinations (Noordsy et al. 1991);
- Depressive symptoms (Drake et al. 1989);
- Disruptive behaviors (Alterman et al. 1980; Drake et al. 1989);
- Assaultiveness (Yesavage and Zarcone 1983);
- Poor self-care (Alterman et al. 1980; Drake et al. 1989);
- Housing instability and homelessness (Drake et al. 1989, 1991);
- Treatment noncompliance (Alterman et al. 1980; Drake et al. 1989; Osher et al., in press);
- Increased rates of other drug abuse (Barbee et al. 1989; Drake et al. 1989; Osher et al., in press; Test et al. 1989); and
- Increased rates of rehospitalization and incarceration (Drake et al. 1989; Osher et al., in press).

Use of other drugs, particularly marijuana, stimulants, and psychedelics, has been associated with exacerbation of positive symptoms of psychosis (Knudsen and Vilmar 1984; Negrete et al. 1986; Treffert 1978) and with increased rates of hospitalization (Craig et al. 1985; Richard et al. 1985) in people with diagnosed schizophrenia. In addition, there is evidence that these drugs may induce schizophrenia in previously unaffected individuals. McLellan and colleagues (1979) found, for example, that primary stimulant abusers who appeared psychologically normal during their first admission for drug abuse treatment but who continued to abuse stimulants developed psychotic symptoms that were increasingly refractory to treatment over time; after 6 years, they were indistinguishable from patients diagnosed as chronic schizophrenic. Breakey and colleagues (1974) found that individuals with schizophrenia who were drug abusers had become ill at an earlier age but had better premorbid adjustment than schizophrenic individuals who did not abuse drugs.

Although the use of alcohol and other drugs is sometimes associated with positive effects, particularly according to self-report, the short-term effects of these substances appear to be predominantly negative (Dixon et al. 1990). Although we know little about the long-term effects of alcohol and other drugs on the course of schizophrenic illness (Turner and Tsuang 1990), it seems likely that their long-term effects are also quite negative because of the cumulative risks of illness exacerbation, homelessness, violence, and exposure to HIV-infected drug addicts.

Homelessness

Homelessness is increasingly a psychiatric as well as a social problem (Bachrach 1987; Bassuk et al. 1984; Levine 1984; Roth et al. 1986). Treatment alternatives in the community are totally dependent on the availability of adequate housing, but in many U.S. cities only 5% to 10% of the necessary housing units are available to the mental health system (Mechanic and Aiken 1987). The result is a burgeoning population of homeless mentally ill people. Prevalence estimates from several U.S. cities indicate that between 500,000 and 1 million of the 1.5 to 3 million homeless Americans are mentally ill (Levine 1984). With the further loss of low-income housing, the situation worsens continually.

Surveys of the homeless using structured diagnostic interviews indicate that schizophrenia is a common diagnosis among these people (Breakey et al. 1989; Koegel et al. 1988; Susser et al. 1989). In the Los Angeles study, for example, 13% of the homeless had a lifetime diagnosis of schizophrenia (Koegel et al. 1988). Other psychiatric diagnoses were also common among the homeless, but the rate of schizophrenia among homeless people relative to domiciled people in the Los Angeles ECA study was the highest of any diagnosis.

Although there are few longitudinal data, homeless mentally ill people have several characteristics that suggest an adverse long-term course (Lamb 1984; Tessler and Dennis 1989). They typically exhibit severe psychiatric symptoms, abuse of alcohol and other drugs, a variety of general medical problems, and an inability to provide for their basic needs. They generally do not receive the services that are warranted by their condition (Farr et al. 1986; Rossi et al. 1986). It seems likely that the debilitating effects of exposure, victimization, and untreated alcohol, drug, mental health, and general medical problems would lead to severe morbidity and early mortality (Institute of Medicine 1988).

Conclusions

Many sociocultural changes in recent years have combined to expose young people with schizophrenia to severe hazards that complicate their adjustment to severe mental illness and their transition to adulthood. These changes may be adversely affecting the long-term outcomes of the cohort of people with schizophrenia in the postinstitutional generation. It is unclear to what degree future long-term follow-up research will continue to yield optimistic results, because the relatively positive long-term outcomes among previous cohorts of individuals with schizophrenia may not generalize to younger cohorts. The following conclusions can be drawn about the long-term course of young people with schizophrenia in today's America:

1. In the postinstitutional era, treatment is often nonexistent or fragmented, underfunded, and incomplete. Because psychiatric and medical treatments are often separated from social welfare services, even those in treatment may not receive the social services necessary to meet basic needs.
2. In addition to inadequate treatment, people with schizophrenia who are in the community are exposed to a variety of stresses that threaten their survival and ability to make an optimal adjustment. These include frequent exposure to alcohol and other drugs, shunting to jails and prisons, and homelessness.
3. Longitudinal research is urgently needed to understand the long-term impact of these and other social hazards on individuals with schizophrenia who are in the community. Researchers should be sensitive to cohort effects, because exposure to social hazards is likely to be more deleterious for those in large urban areas, and for younger people who are learning to adjust to mental illness and who are making the transition to adulthood.

4. To protect the schizophrenic individual's potential for significant long-term improvement, mental health administrators, providers, and service researchers need to pay rigorous attention to the social hazards that threaten such an individual's adaptation.

References

Alterman AI, Erdlen FR, McLellan AT, et al: Problem drinking in hospitalized schizophrenic patients. Addiction Behavior 5:273–276, 1980

Bachrach LL: Young adult chronic patients: an analytical review of the literature. Hosp Community Psychiatry 33:189–197, 1982

Bachrach LL: Issues in identifying and treating the homeless mentally ill, in Leona Bachrach Speaks: Selected Speeches and Lectures (New Directions for Mental Health Services, No. 35). Edited by Bachrach LL. San Francisco, CA, Jossey-Bass, 1987

Barbee JG, Clark PD, Craqanzo MS, et al: Alcohol and substance abuse among schizophrenic patients presenting to an emergency service. J Nerv Ment Dis 177:400–407, 1989

Barber JW, Kerler R, Kellogg EJ, et al: Clinical and demographic characteristics of chronic inpatients: implications for treatment and research. Psychiatr Q 53:257–270, 1988

Bassuk EL, Rubin L, Lauriat A: Is homelessness a mental health problem? Am J Psychiatry 141:1546–1550, 1984

Boyd JH, Burke JD, Gruenberg E, et al: Exclusion criteria of DSM-III. Arch Gen Psychiatry 41:983–989, 1984

Breakey WR, Goodell H, Lorenz PC, et al: Hallucinogenic drugs as precipitants of schizophrenia. Psychol Med 4:255–261, 1974

Breakey WR, Fischer PJ, Kramer M, et al: Health and mental health problems of homeless men and women in Baltimore. JAMA 262:1352–1357, 1989

Caton CLM: The new chronic patient and the system of community care. Hosp Community Psychiatry 32:475–478, 1981

Craig TJ, Lin SP, El-Defrawi MH, et al: Clinical correlates of readmission in a schizophrenic cohort. Psychiatr Q 57:5–10, 1985

Dixon L, Haas G, Weiden P, et al: Acute effects of drug abuse in schizophrenic patients: clinical observations and patients' self-reports. Schizophr Bull 16:69–79, 1990

Drake RE, Osher FC, Wallach MA: Alcohol use and abuse in schizophrenia: a prospective community study. J Nerv Ment Dis 177:408–414, 1989

Drake RE, Osher FC, Noordsy DL, et al: Diagnosis of alcohol use disorders in schizophrenia. Schizophr Bull 16:57–67, 1990

Drake RE, Wallach MA, Teague GB, et al: Housing instability and homelessness among rural schizophrenic patients. Am J Psychiatry 148:330–336, 1991

Elder GH: History and the life course, in Transitions: The Family and the Life Course. Edited by Hareven T. New York, Academic, 1978

Elder GH: Military times and turning points in men's lives. Developmental Psychology 22:233–245, 1986

Elder GH, Van Nguyen T, Caspi A: Linking family hardship to children's lives. Child Dev 56:361–375, 1985

Farr RK, Koegel P, Burnam A: A Study of Homelessness and Mental Illness in the Skid Row Area of Los Angeles. Los Angeles, CA, County Department of Mental Health, 1986

Feinstein AF: Clinical Biostatistics. St. Louis, MO, CV Mosby, 1977

Goldman HH, Feder J, Scanlon W: Chronic mental patients in nursing homes: reexamining data from the national nursing home survey. Hosp Community Psychiatry 37:269–272, 1986

Institute of Medicine: Homelessness, Health, and Human Needs. Washington, DC, National Academy Press, 1988

Katz HM, Frank A, Gunderson JG, et al: Psychotherapy of schizophrenia: what happens to treatment dropouts? J Nerv Ment Dis 172:326–331, 1984

Knudsen P, Vilmar T: Cannabis and neuroleptic agents in schizophrenia. Acta Psychiatr Scand 69:162–174, 1984

Koegel P, Burnam A, Farr RK: The prevalence of specific psychiatric disorders among homeless individuals in the inner city of Los Angeles. Arch Gen Psychiatry 45:1085–1092, 1988

Lamb HR: Young adult chronic patients: the new drifters. Hosp Community Psychiatry 33:465–468, 1982

Lamb HR (ed): The Homeless Mentally Ill. Washington, DC, American Psychiatric Association, 1984

Leighton DC, Harding JS, Macklin DB, et al: The Character of Danger. New York, Basic Books, 1963

Levine IS: Homelessness: its implications for mental health policy and practice. Psychosocial Rehabilitation Journal 8:6–16, 1984

McLellan AT, Woody GE, O'Brien CP: Development of psychiatric illness in drug abusers. N Engl J Med 301:1310–1314, 1979

Mechanic D, Aiken LH: Improving the care of patients with chronic mental illness. N Engl J Med 317:1634–1638, 1987

Minkoff K: Beyond deinstitutionalization: a new ideology for the postinstitutional era. Hosp Community Psychiatry 38:945–950, 1987

National Institute on Drug Abuse: National Household Survey on Drug Abuse: Population Estimates, 1985 (DHHS Publ No ADM-87-1539). Rockville, MD, National Institute on Drug Abuse, 1987

Negrete JC, Knapp WP, Douglas DE, et al: Cannabis affects the severity of schizophrenic symptoms: results of a clinical survey. Psychol Med 16:515–520, 1986

Noordsy DL, Drake RE, Teague GB, et al: Subjective experiences related to alcohol use among schizophrenics. J Nerv Ment Dis 179:410–414, 1991

Osher FC, Drake RE, Noordsy DL, et al: Correlates and outcomes of alcohol use disorder among rural schizophrenics. (in press)

Pepper B, Kirshner MC, Ryglewicz H: The young adult chronic patient: overview of a population. Hosp Community Psychiatry 32:463–469, 1981

Regier DA, Burke JD: Psychiatric disorders in the community: the Epidemiologic Catchment Area study, in Psychiatry Update: American Psychiatric Association Annual Review, Vol 6. Edited by Hales RE, Frances AJ. Washington, DC, American Psychiatric Press, 1987

Regier DA, Farmer ME, Ray DS, et al: Comorbidity of mental disorders with alcohol and other drug abuse. JAMA 119:2511–2518, 1990

Richard ML, Liskow BI, Perry PJ: Recent psychostimulant use in hospitalized schizophrenics. J Clin Psychiatry 135:79–83, 1985

Richardson MA, Craig TJ, Haugland G: Treatment patterns of young chronic schizophrenic patients in the era of deinstitutionalization. Psychiatr Q 57:104–110, 1985

Rossi PH, Fisher GA, Willis G: The Condition of the Homeless of Chicago. Amherst, MA, University of Massachusetts Social and Demographic Research Institute, 1986

Roth D, Bean GJ, Hyde PS: Homelessness and mental health policy: developing an appropriate role for the 1980s. Community Ment Health J 22:203–214, 1986

Schneier FR, Siris SG: A review of psychoactive substance use and abuse in schizophrenia: patterns of drug choice. J Nerv Ment Dis 175:641–652, 1987

Stanton AH, Gunderson JG, Knapp PH, et al: Effects of psychotherapy on schizophrenic patients, I: the design and implementation of a controlled study. Schizophr Bull 10:520–563, 1984

Stewart AJ, Healy JM: Linking individual development and social changes. Am Psychol 44:30–42, 1989

Stroul BA: Community support systems for persons with long-term mental illness: a conceptual framework. Psychosocial Rehabilitation Journal 12:9–26, 1989

Susser E, Struening EL, Conover S: Psychiatric problems in homeless men. Arch Gen Psychiatry 46:845–850, 1989

Tessler RC, Dennis DL: A synthesis of NIMH-funded research concerning persons who are homeless and mentally ill. Rockville, MD, National Institute of Mental Health, 1989

Test MA, Knoedler WH, Allness DJ, et al: Characteristics of young adults with schizophrenic disorders treated in the community. Hosp Community Psychiatry 36:853–858, 1985

Test MA, Wallisch LS, Allness DJ, et al: Substance use in young adults with schizophrenic disorders. Schizophr Bull 15:465–476, 1989

Treffert DA: Marijuana use in schizophrenia: a clear hazard. Am J Psychiatry 135:1213–1215, 1978

Turner WM, Tsuang MT: Impact of substance abuse on the course and outcome of schizophrenia. Schizophr Bull 16:87–95, 1990

Von Korff M, Nestadt G, Romanoski A, et al: Prevalence of treated and untreated DSM-III schizophrenia: results of a two-stage community survey. J Nerv Ment Dis 173:577–581, 1985

Yesavage JA, Zarcone V: History of drug abuse and dangerous behavior in inpatient schizophrenics. J Clin Psychiatry 44:259–261, 1983

4

Implications for the Pharmacotherapy of Schizophrenia

The introduction in the 1950s of chlorpromazine as a treatment for psychosis created a turning point in the field of psychiatry. Suddenly, pharmacological agents known as neuroleptics or antipsychotics were available to counteract the most flagrant aspects of psychosis: hallucinations, delusions, fragmented thinking, and various grossly disordered or bizarre behaviors. The expansion of large psychiatric hospitals financed by state funds diminished as these institutions began to release previously "intractable" patients. Insulin shock therapy, electroconvulsive therapy, lobotomy, and reserpine, previously used with some desperation in the attempt to treat people with schizophrenia, fell into disuse. Optimism was revived and soon "community psychiatry," "deinstitutionalization," and "patients' rights" became watchwords of the times.

However, despite the miraculous changes brought about by neuroleptic medications, major problems remain. Indeed, there is much more to schizophrenia than simply psychosis, and the most challenging problems we now face have to do with those aspects of the disorder.

That schizophrenia is a long-term process has been recognized for many years. That this process might involve more than just the acute psychotic manifestations of the illness, however, was not so clear until drugs existed that could curb the psychotic symptomatology. Enthusiasm for the capacity of neuroleptic drugs to tame this symptomatology was initially so great that the very definition of schizophrenia came to rely heavily on the observation of flagrant but potentially drug-responsive psychotic symptoms. For almost three decades, the circular logic created by this situation kept a focus on the acute psychotic manifestations of schizophrenia. Many clinicians even became convinced that they were successfully treating this illness when those manifestations were suppressed.

Over time it has become clear, however, that containing psychosis is only the first step in treating schizophrenia. This step must be followed by a process that aims at broader healing of the patient as a person. Thus, clinicians must now address how best to promote the recovery process. This chapter reviews some ways in which medications, particularly neuroleptic medications, can help individuals with schizophrenia. It describes aspects of both acute treatment and maintenance treatment, with attention to adverse medication effects that impair the quality of life, reduce the capacity to relate to others, and interfere with treatment compliance. Then we offer suggestions for improving the treatment of schizophrenia through new medications or through new methods of using previously available medications.

The Acute Phase of Pharmacotherapy for Schizophrenia

Pharmacotherapy of patients with schizophrenia can be divided into acute and maintenance phases. In this schema, an abrupt increase in symptoms would be treated as an acute episode, whether it represents the onset of a new psychotic disorder or an exacerbation of a chronic schizophrenic illness. In contrast, the alleviation of chronic symptoms and the use of medication prophylactically against relapse are examples of treatment in the maintenance phase.

In the acute phase, the goal of pharmacotherapy is usually to control disruptive or maladaptive behavior, reestablish consensually validated belief systems, normalize the processes of perception, and restore a patient's baseline level of functioning. Neuroleptics are particularly helpful in reducing hallucinations, suspiciousness, mannerisms, hyperactivity, and loud behavior (Neborsky et al. 1987). When a patient is out of control and may harm himself or herself or others, alleviation of these symptoms through prompt use of neuroleptic medication is a helpful and even a potentially lifesaving intervention.

Rapid Tranquilization

Emergent disruptive behavior often responds well to the acute administration of neuroleptic medication, an intervention termed either *rapid tranquilization* or *focal neuroleptization.* Dubin and colleagues (1986) have emphasized the distinction between this intervention and *rapid neuroleptization,* which is an attempt to accelerate the remission of a patient's core psychotic symptoms by initiating neuroleptic treatment with large loading doses.

Although rapid neuroleptization has been shown to be ineffective at reducing length of hospitalization or improving long-term response to treatment, rapid tranquilization can be highly effective at establishing behavioral control in the emergency setting and is therefore a powerful use of neuroleptic medication (Dubin et al. 1986; Ellison and Jacobs 1986). A series of studies carried out in the past decade have helped to provide guidelines for indications, route of administration, dosage, and choice of drug (Adams 1984; Escobar et al. 1983; Kirkpatrick and Burnett 1982; Neborsky et al. 1987; Schaffer et al. 1982).

Rapid tranquilization is indicated when a psychotic patient's behavior presents a danger of harm to self or others and is unresponsive to alternative approaches, such as talking or offering food. Physical restraints may be tried either before or after neuroleptic usage, depending on the characteristics of the patient and the treatment setting.

During rapid tranquilization, medication is often administered intramuscularly but can also be administered in pill or liquid form (Dubin et al. 1986). Pharmacokinetic considerations argue against administering oral doses more often than hourly. Even in high dosages, neuroleptic use in rapid tranquilization during the phase of illness marked by a florid inception of psychotic symptomatology is usually without serious adverse effects (Tesar et al. 1985). Doses that would have been considered low in past decades, however, are now recommended as potentially effective even in this acute setting. Neborsky and others (1987), for example, found that acutely hospitalized psychotic patients who received either 2 mg or 10 mg of intramuscular haloperidol (Haldol) showed considerable reduction in hyperactivity and hostility when rated after 1 hour.

The neuroleptic medications usually preferred in rapid tranquilization are the high-potency ones such as haloperidol (Haldol), fluphenazine (Prolixin), thiothixene (Navane), or loxapine (Loxitane). These drugs produce oversedation and hypotension less frequently than lower potency neuroleptics. They do, however, cause acute dystonic reactions (muscle spasm) fairly often. In fact, Boyer and colleagues (1987) reported almost uniform induction of acute dystonia (muscle spasm) by haloperidol in a group of psychotic patients composed mostly of young males. In young psychotic males or patients with a history of neuroleptic-induced acute dystonia, prophylactic anticholinergic medication is indicated during rapid tranquilization (Boyer et al. 1987).

To minimize side effects and maximize therapeutic effects of rapid tranquilization, researchers have suggested several new modifications of the technique. The potentiation of a neuroleptic injection by a concurrent injection of the benzodiazepine lorazepam (Ativan) has been described in agitated psychotic or mentally retarded patients by Dubin and colleagues (1986) and by Salzman and colleagues (1986) in a psychiatric intensive care unit. The concurrent intramuscular administration of one such regimen—5 mg of haloperidol combined with 1 mg of lorazepam—has become increasingly popular among psychiatric emergency services. Many clinicians find that this approach achieves excellent control of disruptive psychotic symptoms while producing less affective dulling, acute dystonic symptomatology, or oversedation.

A controversial new alternative to rapid tranquilization with neuroleptics employs midazolam (Versed), a potent and short-acting benzodiazepine that can induce a brief state of intense sedation in aggressive, hostile, or severely agitated psychotic patients (Mendoza et al. 1987). Because there is some controversy over whether midazolam can produce respiratory depression of clinical significance (Dixon 1985), it should be used for rapid tranquilization only when resuscitation equipment is readily available. This is so especially when the patient has pulmonary disease or may have taken other central nervous system (CNS) depressant chemicals.

Limitations of Neuroleptics

Clinicians who work with individuals diagnosed as schizophrenic must avoid relying exclusively on neuroleptic medications when treating the illness's acute psychotic manifestations. Sometimes medication issues, such as inadequate prior pharmacotherapy or noncompliance with a prescribed regime of medications, result in the emergence of psychotic symptoms. At other times, however, a psychotic exacerbation reflects subtle shifts in the patient's psychosocial environment. Unexpected or overly stressful life events can alter the precarious balance of functioning in an already impaired individual. When this is so, the use of medications for rapid tranquilization has important limitations and even potential adverse effects. Medications will not alter the patient's psychosocial environment directly and may even delay recognition of an important stressor.

In the worst scenario, neuroleptic medications used aggressively during the acute phase of a psychotic illness can produce adverse effects that undermine their therapeutic actions and interfere with long-term treatment compliance. Unwanted sedation, for example, may weaken a patient's capacity to sort through behavioral alternatives or understand fully a complex life situation. An acute dystonic reaction or a dysphoric mood reaction may give an already stressed patient yet another problem with which to struggle. These adverse effects may produce in the patient an aversion to further neuroleptic treatment. Pharmacotherapy, therefore, must be integrated into a broader psychosocial approach to treatment.

Intermittent Dosing

A pioneering strategy for dealing with acute decompensations in patients with chronic schizophrenia is called *targeted* or *intermittent dosing* and has been advocated by Carpenter and colleagues (1985). Clinicians who espouse this approach maintain that some patients with schizophrenia who are only mildly symptomatic may remain in remission without medication for significant lengths of time. During these periods, the underlying schizophrenic process is apparently quiescent. This approach, which depends upon close monitoring, usually by social supports as well as treatment staff, allows some people with schizophrenia to refrain from taking neuroleptics during times of symptom remission.

The intermittent approach was built on the earlier observations of Herz and Melville (1980), that many patients exhibit characteristic signs or symptoms during the early stages of relapse. Patients or family members were found capable of observing these signs and of predicting a relapse with considerable accuracy. Carpenter and colleagues (1985) incorporated these observations into a treatment protocol that allowed patients to remain unmedicated until the occurrence of relapse symptoms. Patients treated in this way increase their level of responsibility for obtaining treatment, as well as their own real and perceived mastery with regard to their condition. At the same time, their lower total intake of neuroleptic medication results in fewer adverse medication effects, both acutely and chronically.

Effects of Gender and Age

Patients' response to neuroleptic medications is modified by gender and age. In four studies that examine the effects of gender, a total of nearly 600 females diagnosed as schizophrenic were compared to as many males with this disorder (Dworkin and Adams 1984; Kolakowska et al. 1985; Seeman 1983; Young and Meltzer 1980). In each study, women responded more quickly to lower doses of neuroleptics and were stabilized at lower doses than were the men. This effect may be age-related, as the difference between the genders decreases after women reach age 40. Estrogens can counteract the effects of dopamine, a neurotransmitter that in excess may aggravate psychotic symptoms. One hypothetical explanation of this gender difference, therefore, is that the higher levels of estrogens found in women under age 40 may delay the onset of schizophrenic symptoms, mute their intensity, and partially protect the individual during pregnancy, while also exacerbating the risk of some acute or delayed adverse motoric effects of neuroleptic treatment (Seeman 1982).

The Maintenance Phase of Pharmacotherapy for Schizophrenia

The maintenance or prophylactic phase of treatment begins following an acute episode. Although the true nature of the prophylactic effects of neuroleptics remains controversial, the work of Hogarty and others (1974) has clearly established that individuals with schizophrenia on long-term antipsychotic medication undergo fewer symptomatic exacerbations. Studies in which patients with schizophrenia were randomly switched, in a double-blind manner, from active medication to placebo have shown a consistently high rate of relapse. Even when patients have been in remission on medication for 2 to 3 years, the relapse rate during the first 12 months off medication approaches 65% (Baldessarini 1985). For patients emerging from an initial episode of schizophrenia, a similarly high relapse rate has been noted when pharmacotherapy is not sustained (Kane 1987).

Beyond their prophylactic role, antipsychotic medications serve to suppress persistent positive symptoms (that is, hallucinations, delusions, and thinking disturbances) in patients diagnosed as having chronic schizophrenia. There is even evidence that some patients experience increasing levels of symptom relief when antipsychotic medications are continued over a period of months after the acute phase of illness (Osser 1988). However, the long-term usefulness of currently available neuroleptics in the treatment of patients with schizophrenia is limited by noncompliance and side effects.

Noncompliance

Medication noncompliance is a primary concern during long-term treatment or the maintenance phase of schizophrenia. Similar to other patients with a chronic illness, approximately one-half of all patients with schizophrenia are noncompliant with their medication regimens (Kane 1985; Young et al. 1986). Moreover, failure to adhere to medication regimen is a major factor in relapse and rehospitalization among schizophrenic patients (Hogarty and Goldberg 1973; Mason et al. 1963; Van Putten and May 1978a). Noncompliance has been related to lack of social supports, denial of illness, grandiosity, early subjective response to medications, medication side effects, poor treatment alliance, and substance abuse (Bartko et al. 1988; Drake et al. 1989; Kane 1985; Young et al. 1986). Programs to improve medication compliance have addressed each of these problems, often by increasing the patient's involvement in making decisions about and monitoring medications (i.e., by improving medication management skills; Eckman et al. 1990). Addressing medication side effects, which we will discuss in the next section, merits particular attention as a critical aspect of this process.

Side Effects of Long-Term Neuroleptic Use

In the years since formulation of the dopamine hypothesis of schizophrenia (Meltzer and Stahl 1976), neuroleptic medications have been chosen and developed for their ability to block receptors that bind this neurotransmitter in the brain. Overwhelming evidence associates dopaminergic blockade not only with the suppression of acute psychotic symptomatology (Klein et al. 1980) but also, when maintained longitudinally, with remarkably effective protection against the recurrence of acute psychotic symptoms (Davis 1985a, 1985b). An unwanted by-product of treatment with these medications, however, is the blockage of brain dopaminergic receptors other than the ones most directly involved in the manifestation of psychosis. This incidental blockade produces some of the most tenacious and disturbing side effects of neuroleptics.

Some of these side effects are easily recognized and clearly attributable to the use of medications. Tremor, muscular rigidity, and dystonia have been linked to acute dopaminergic blockade in the part of the brain that controls nonvoluntary movements, the extrapyramidal system. *Tardive dyskinesia,* also an extrapyramidal side effect, but one which tends to be associated with long-term neuroleptic exposure, is perhaps the most feared neuroleptic side effect (Woerner et al. 1991). This is so because the associated mouth and tongue movements in severe cases can be quite disfiguring and are often irreversible. Rhythmic hand or foot movements or even hip or back movements can also be manifestations of tardive dyskinesia.

Other more subtle side effects of medications, however, are often misunderstood and mistaken for depression, anxiety, or manifestations of schizophrenia. These effects are potentially devastating. They are caused by the very medications that were meant to help bring these patients more easily into contact with others. Instead, added symptoms increase the isolating barrier that separates them from the surrounding world. Two of the most disabling subtle adverse effects of neuroleptics are akinesia and akathisia, which can more easily be missed or misinterpreted and are therefore singled out here for special consideration.

Akinesia. Akinesia, a reduction of movements, has increasingly become recognized as an important neuroleptic side effect, especially prevalent in patients who take neuroleptics on a long-term basis. One confusing issue is that the term akinesia has been used in more than one way over the years. Initially the term was used to denote reduced accessory muscle movements, such as limitation of the normal arm swing when walking. Most clinicians learn easily to take note of the shuffling, robotic, "neurolepticized look" of patients manifesting this form of akinesia. To treat patients adequately, clinicians should first be able to recognize the adverse effect and then respond either by reducing the neuroleptic dosage or by increasing the antiparkinsonian treatment, whichever is more appropriate.

More subtle, however, are the manifestations of akinesia that affect small muscle function more than accessory motor function in large muscle groups. When the face or vocal cords are affected, the patient can be left with a less emotionally expressive face, even a "bland," "stupid-looking," or "out-of-it" appearance. The voice may sound monotonous or indifferent. This side effect can be extremely damaging socially, because so many subtle cues in social interactions—such as attention, interest, understanding, need for further information or elaboration, friendliness, and trust—are mediated through facial expression and tone of voice.

Patients who, on the basis of a medication side effect, communicate poorly in this crucial nonverbal realm are at a distinct disadvantage. Who would want to hire such a person? Who would want to introduce such a person as a member of his or her family? Who would want to go out on a date with such a person? Even worse, people in daily contact with the patient usually fail to recognize the actual source of the problem: the friends don't know, the family doesn't know, the employer doesn't know. In fact, even the patient and physician may fail to realize the true nature of the problem. It would be challenging enough to try to cope with such a problem even with knowledge of its medical origin. It is even more difficult to deal with this condition when its cause is unknown. Often the withdrawn or expressionless attitude of an akinetic patient is attributed to a psychological cause, to some sort of emotional "deficit," or to an inherent lack of capacity for rapport.

Another potentially devastating manifestation of akinesia is the lack of spontaneity that can occur on an extrapyramidal basis as a neuroleptic side effect (Rifkin et al. 1975; Siris 1987; Van Putten and May 1978b).

Patients suffering this side effect behave as if their "starter motor is broken." As they sit in a chair and watch television, for example, they lack the spontaneity to turn it off and do something else, or even to change the channel when the show ends. Instead, they sit passively, witnessing whatever comes on next, no matter how uninteresting or unappealing. Although they will answer questions when asked or participate in activities when urged, patients with this side effect tend not to initiate conversations or activities themselves, even ones they might find pleasurable or interesting. This manifestation of akinesia easily can be missed or misunderstood by all concerned as a deficit in motivation or drive or as an intrinsic deterioration in social skills and cognitive processes. Again, who would want such a person for a friend? And, again, who would wish to see such qualities (or lack of qualities) in himself or herself, especially without having a clear idea of how they came about or what to do about them?

What to do about them, of course, is to decrease neuroleptic medication if possible. Some patients and family members might even prefer the presence of mild psychotic symptoms in this phase of the disorder to the sometimes more disabling symptoms of akinesia. If neuroleptic drugs cannot be further reduced, either because of psychotic symptoms or because of an unacceptable risk of their reemergence, antiparkinsonian medications should be added in higher dosages to counteract akinesia. Sometimes a lack of evidence of even mild anticholinergic side effects such as dry mouth despite an apparently adequate antiparkinsonian medication dosage indicates that these medications are being metabolized at an unusually high rate. There is a tenfold variability in the rate at which different individuals metabolize anticholinergic antiparkinsonian drugs (Tune and Coyle 1980). Therefore, in the absence of side effects and in the possible presence of akinesia, antiparkinsonian medication should be pushed to higher than standard levels (up to 10 to 12 mg a day of benztropine [Cogentin], or its equivalent). Even if some peripheral anticholinergic side effects occur, they can be counteracted with drugs such as bethanechol, pilocarpine eyedrops, or both.

Most patients who are experiencing akinesia will respond rapidly, within a few days to a week, to antiparkinsonian medication. An ineffective trial of antiparkinsonian medication, therefore, need not be prolonged. Because akinesia is so impairing and so correctable, it is a very unfortunate side effect to leave untreated.

Akathisia. Another extrapyramidal neuroleptic side effect that may occur in a subtle form is akathisia, a syndrome of motoric restlessness that can be drug induced (Barnes and Braude 1985; Braude et al. 1983; Siris 1985; Stahl 1985; Van Putten 1975; Van Putten et al. 1984). Gross akathisia has been well described. It makes patients pace, fidget, and feel restless. By and large, clinicians have been trained to recognize this uncomfortable state in patients. Subtle akathisia, on the other hand, can be difficult to recognize. As subclinical restlessness, it manifests as a predisposition to behavior and action. It can be quite uncomfortable, making patients feel dysphoric or even desperate. In a way, it can be thought of as the opposite side of the coin from akinesia: these patients' "starter motors" refuse to turn off.

A symptom such as akathisia tends to get patients into trouble. They may say things better left unsaid, do or try things better left undone, or wander restlessly into someone else's "space," figuratively or even literally. Obviously, these are not traits that will increase a person's popularity. Even worse, the unacceptability of these behaviors is compounded when all involved, including the patient, fail to recognize the source of the problem, attributing it instead to dynamic motivations, weakness of self-control, innate lack of tact, or other developmental or psychological factors.

Akathisia, unfortunately, is not always easy to treat. Maximal reduction of neuroleptic medication is, of course, the first step. Amantadine or other anticholinergic medications may sometimes be helpful, though often they are not. Benzodiazepines may reduce akathisia in some individuals, as may propranolol or other beta adrenergic blocker medications (Adler et al. 1985, 1986; Fleishhacker et al. 1990; Gelenberg 1987; Lipinski et al. 1984).

The problem of negative symptoms. Clearly, neuroleptic medications can have unfortunate counterproductive effects on individuals with schizophrenia over the long term. Some of these effects can even be attributed mistakenly to schizophrenia itself, prompting an increase rather than a decrease in medications. Even when neuroleptics are used judiciously, their effects on certain schizophrenic symptoms can be disappointingly limited. Their effects are especially unsatisfactory in treating the persistent and debilitating chronic deficit symptoms collectively termed "negative symptoms."

This term describes those deficits in normal functioning that patients with schizophrenia so often experience over the life course of their illness (Andreasen and Olsen 1982; Carpenter et al. 1985, 1988; Crow 1980; Pogue-Geile and Zubin 1988; Sommers 1985; Walker and Lewine 1988). These include deficits in a range of characteristics, including affective range and responsiveness, thinking, speech regulation, interest, capacity for pleasure, motivation, perseverance, and attention. It is unclear whether such a heterogeneous group of symptoms can truly be attributed to a common etiology or pathophysiology. More likely, a variety of biological, psychopharmacological, psychological, and social factors are at play in the development of these negative symptoms.

Researchers have advanced various hypotheses in an attempt to unify the concept of negative symptoms with other theories about schizophrenia. The most prevalent neurotransmitter hypothesis concerning the etiology of negative symptoms involves a proposed state of dopaminergic hypofunction (Meltzer 1985). This theory integrates well with the dopaminergic hypothesis of schizophrenia. The period of psychosis can be understood as a dopaminergic "storm" that is later followed by a period (usually lengthier) of dopaminergic hypofunction, perhaps even dopaminergic burnout as a result of neuronal damage or neuronal death. The clinical manifestations of this hypofunctional state could include many of the so-called negative symptoms.

The implications of this theory for neuroleptic maintenance and prophylaxis are profound. Would patients with negative symptoms do better without neuroleptic medications, if the neuroleptic could be further compromising their already impaired dopaminergic functioning? Perhaps some would; however, the data do reveal that the risk of psychotic relapse is high once neuroleptic treatment ceases (Andrews et al. 1976; Davis 1985a, 1985b; Davis and Andriukaitis 1986; Hogarty 1984; Hogarty et al. 1974; Kane et al. 1983; Lieberman et al. 1986; Prien et al. 1971). With relapse comes the attendant risk of further damage: psychological, social, financial, and perhaps neuronal. Ultimately, patients with prominent negative symptoms may receive treatment with adjunctive dopaminergic agonists such as L-dopa or bromocriptine. Reports of the safety and efficacy of these approaches, however, remain largely anecdotal (Cutler et al. 1984; Levi-Minzi et al., in press; Ludatscher 1989; Meltzer et al. 1986).

Many patients with schizophrenia have discovered the hazards inherent in excessive neuroleptic dosing. Whether it is concern about akinesia, akathisia, negative symptoms, or some other dysphoric experience attendant to neuroleptic use that motivates them, patients often express a resistance to the use of these drugs (Kane 1985; Van Putten 1974). This is not a situation in which power struggles are likely to be fruitful. Instead, the patient's active participation in the medication process must be encouraged. When patient and physician share their expertise and experience, they can collaborate on a reasonable plan in their attempt to steer between the Scylla of psychosis and the Charybdis of negative symptoms and other undesirable effects. A failure of this collaboration can trigger noncompliance and estrangement, leading to renewed psychosis and further deterioration.

Psychosocial effects. Another important aspect of schizophrenia, in addition to negative symptoms, that is not addressed by currently available pharmacotherapy is the effects of adverse psychosocial circumstances on the patient's mental status. This aspect has been particularly identified in the body of expressed emotion (EE) research, which has emphasized how an environment rich in hostile expressed emotion can undermine the effectiveness of neuroleptic treatment. In a study conducted by Vaughn and colleagues (1984), for example, "no patient with a low EE score who was taking medication regularly had a relapse during the [9-month] follow-up period," whereas a significant minority of patients with high EE scores (as many as 44%) had relapses while taking medication (pp. 1174, 1175). This finding was supported by Strang and colleagues (1981), who reported that their group of patients from high EE environments relapsed less frequently when they were taking medications, had more limited contact with family members, and were attending family therapy meetings.

A further issue that pharmacotherapy alone cannot solve in the treatment of schizophrenia arises from the existential disappointment faced by many psychotic patients who attempt to grapple with the meaning of having a chronic and severe mental illness. Medications may help to stabilize a patient's mental status, allowing psychotherapeutic work to progress more easily, but they should not be relied on to obliterate awareness of sources of stress (Osser 1988) or to dull a patient into a passive, compliant state. Reliance on medication may be of greatest value early in the course of illness or during acute exacerbation, whereas cautiously lowering doses later on may allow a patient to be more accessible to psychosocial interventions.

From a psychotherapeutic viewpoint, exclusive reliance on pharmacotherapy may also adversely affect the longitudinal treatment of an individual with schizophrenia by communicating a viewpoint about the disorder that emphasizes the patient's passivity in the face of an illness and that ignores the psychosocial components. Instead, clinicians should try to understand the possible source of a symptomatic exacerbation even while they are evaluating the usefulness of pharmacotherapeutic intervention. Osser (1988), for example, has noted that the clinicians' facile use of "prn" (as needed) medications can aid a patient in distancing himself or herself from the psychosocial context of symptoms rather than leading to a focus on stressors and improving the means of coping with them psychologically.

Possibilities for Improving Maintenance Pharmacotherapy

In the maintenance or prophylactic pharmacotherapy of patients with schizophrenia, suppression of positive symptoms is too limited an objective. Suggestions for improving treatment, in addition to addressing compliance issues, can be divided into three categories: new strategies for using currently available medications, use of medications currently being investigated, and psychosocial aspects of pharmacotherapy.

New Strategies for Current Medications

One important approach to maximizing the long-term benefits of currently available neuroleptics while limiting their adverse effects is the strategy termed *low-dose treatment*. In a representative study, Kane and others (1983) followed stable schizophrenic outpatients during a year of random assignment to a standard or a low dosage of intramuscular fluphenazine decanoate (Prolixin). Though many relapses complicated the lowest dose regimen, the middle dosage (2.5–10 mg intramuscularly every 2 weeks) was associated with a relapse rate of only 24%. Several lines of evidence favored the use of lower dosages despite a higher concomitant relapse rate. The low-dose patients were more easily restabilized during relapse, showed significantly fewer early signs of tardive dyskinesia, and achieved better ratings on some measures of social interaction. Marder and colleagues (1987) found a similar outcome in a 2-year study of patients randomized to receive either 5 mg or 25 mg of fluphenazine decanoate intramuscularly every 2 weeks. Although relapse rates were nearly twice as high in the lower dosage group, the low-dose patients complained of fewer side effects. Symptomatic exacerbations were adequately controlled by small temporary dosage increases.

In addition to the neuroleptics, other currently available medications have been applied to the treatment of schizophrenia. Especially in the treatment of patients with refractory psychosis or other symptoms resistant to conventional treatment, a variety of new approaches are now available. Antidepressants, benzodiazepines, lithium, propranolol, and carbamazepine have each been advocated for specific roles in improving the long-term treatment of individuals with schizophrenia.

The frequent occurrence of depressive symptoms in patients with schizophrenia (Bartels and Drake 1988; Johnson 1981; Knights and Hirsch 1981; Mandel et al. 1982; Martin et al. 1985; McGlashan and Carpenter 1976; Siris et al. 1981, 1987) has raised questions about the potential role of antidepressant medications for these patients. A phenotypic depression doubtless can have a variety of potential etiologies, including akinesia, negative symptoms, situational disappointment, or demoralization. A pragmatic clinical question is whether a depressed schizophrenic patient will respond positively to treatment with an adjunctive antidepressant even if the mood symptoms do not represent a true mood disorder.

The use of antidepressant medications in schizophrenia is still an incompletely studied topic (Siris, in press; Siris et al. 1978). When antidepressants have been given to patients with schizophrenia in the absence of concomitant neuroleptics, exacerbation of psychosis has been reported (Siris et al. 1978). This is not the case, however, when antidepressants are used adjunctly with neuroleptics in such patients. Here, the results of the few reported studies are mixed (Becker 1983; Johnson 1981; Prusoff et al. 1979; Singh et al. 1978; Waehrens and Gerlach 1980). Generally speaking, psychosis has not been seriously exacerbated by antidepressants in this situation if the patients have been otherwise stabilized prior to the addition of the antidepressant. Differences among these studies have involved the specific neuroleptic and antidepressant agents used, dosage and duration of antidepressant treatment, definition of the initial depressed state, and, crucially, the efforts undertaken to eliminate the confounding variable of neuroleptic-induced akinesia. Because almost all the studies reported in the recent literature have used tricyclic antidepressants rather than monoamine oxidase (MAO) inhibitors, it is more difficult to develop conclusions about the latter group.

A reasonable clinical statement is that any patient diagnosed with schizophrenia who is on a stable, moderate dose of neuroleptic, who is not flagrantly psychotic but who exhibits a continuing "depression" syndrome (with such symptoms as anhedonia [incapacity for pleasure], low energy, low self-esteem, pessimism, and an unhappy mood), and who is unresponsive to an aggressive trial of antiparkinsonian medication deserves a full trial of an adequate dose of antidepressant medication added to the neuroleptic and antiparkinsonian drug regime. To minimize the exacerbation of psychotic symptoms, clinicians might be wise to raise the antidepressant gradually to full dosage levels in these patients.

The usefulness of benzodiazepines in schizophrenia requires further study, because they may indeed have a useful role to play. First, they may be useful as an adjunctive treatment in the control of psychosis. Although benzodiazepines administered as the sole antipsychotic agents in schizophrenia are ineffective (Donaldson et al. 1983), they may be useful when added to neuroleptics in the acute control of psychosis, at least for some patients (Dubin et al. 1986; Salzman et al. 1986; Wolkowitz et al. 1988). Much of the work done in this situation has involved lorazepam (Ativan), but other benzodiazepines may be as useful. In some cases, the addition of a benzodiazepine seems to bring the psychosis under control more rapidly than would occur without this drug. It may also benefit a psychotic patient who is in an acutely agitated state by providing sedation. Further studies will be necessary to determine if a benzodiazepine may also reduce the amount of neuroleptic necessary for treatment.

Alprazolam (Xanax) has been tried as a specifically targeted treatment for negative symptoms. Although two early reports detailing alprazolam's effects on small numbers of patients appeared positive (Csernansky et al. 1984; Wolkowitz et al. 1986), a larger controlled trial has failed to substantiate the utility of this approach (Csernansky et al. 1988). However, the final word is not yet in. Neither the initial nor the subsequent trials made an adequate attempt to eliminate the confounding effects of neuroleptic-induced akinesia with antiparkinsonian medication. Therefore, it is possible that there may yet be a role for benzodiazepines in treating negative symptoms.

Of particular interest is the fact that, with the exception of one early trial that appeared positive (Kellner et al. 1975), no attempt has been made to single out individuals with schizophrenia whose illness is characterized by an appearance of anxiety for trials of adjunctive benzodiazepines. This would appear to be a logical strategy. Because one study described patients with negative symptoms as being more worried or phobic (Siris et al. 1988), anxiety reduction could be one way in which benzodiazepines help such patients.

Finally, panic attacks have recently been described in some patients with schizophrenia (Kahn et al. 1988; Sandberg and Siris 1987). It is possible that these attacks might respond to adjunctive antidepressant medication as well (Siris et al. 1989) or perhaps to alternative benzodiazepines (Kahn et al. 1988; Sandberg and Siris 1987). The possibility that a syndrome of agoraphobia in schizophrenia might mistakenly be attributed to the presence of negative symptoms is yet another reason to consider the use of antidepressants or benzodiazepines in devising alternative long-term treatment strategies for suboptimally functioning patients with schizophrenia.

When lithium has proven effective in treating patients diagnosed as having chronic schizophrenia, questions of diagnostic accuracy or specificity have often arisen. At least one study (Donaldson et al. 1983) has suggested that the presence of affective symptoms at the time of diagnosis will not accurately predict whether lithium will prove helpful. Whether affective symptoms are present or absent, these researchers estimate that up to one-third of patients with schizophrenia will show some improvement with lithium as an adjunct to their neuroleptic medication.

Two other medications that have proven helpful in the longer term pharmacotherapy of schizophrenia are propranolol (Inderal and others) and reserpine (Serpasil and others). Given in high doses (even above

3,000 mg per day) with careful monitoring, propranolol has been reported to reduce psychotic symptoms as well as aggressiveness in the presence or absence of neuroleptic medication. Anecdotal reports about propranolol, unfortunately, have been more encouraging than the results from controlled studies (Berlant 1987). In some patients, use of this medication is not feasible because of neurological and cardiovascular side effects (Berlant 1987). Reserpine, which played an important role as an antipsychotic agent prior to the discovery of phenothiazines, has also acquired a limited role as an adjunctive agent in the treatment of refractory psychotic symptoms (Berlant 1986).

Finally, carbamazepine (Tegretol) has been used to treat patients with chronic schizophrenia that appear unresponsive to neuroleptics. As yet, this medication has been insufficiently studied among psychotic patients. In one placebo-controlled study, however, carbamazepine reduced violence and improved symptoms in some patients who showed no prior EEG abnormalities (Dose et al. 1987). Further work in this area is clearly needed.

New Medications

Accompanying the creative use of adjunctive medications, another trend in the improvement of long-term treatment of patients with schizophrenia involves the search for new neuroleptics with superior therapeutic properties. This search is proceeding in two ways: empirical investigations of compounds that are effective, and theory-driven development of new molecules designed to affect dopaminergic pathways suspected to be integral to the pathophysiology of schizophrenia (Tamminga and Gerlach 1987). A current example of a medication that has come into prominence because of its efficacy in previously neuroleptic-refractory schizophrenic patients is clozapine (Clozaril). Its exact mechanism of action is not known, though it has been shown to affect a wide range of nondopaminergic transmitter functions. The purported advantages of clozapine include efficacy in a substantial proportion of previously neuroleptic-resistant schizophrenic patients, low risk of tardive dyskinesia, and low incidence of extrapyramidal side effects. There is a continuing concern regarding the risk of granulocytopenia or agranulocytosis, a potentially fatal complication, which may limit the use of this medication (Marder and Van Putten 1988). Even more limiting, the high cost of clozapine has priced the medication beyond the reach of the large number of patients most in need of it (Pelonero and Elliott 1990).

An example of an investigational drug that attempts to target dopaminergic receptors in the mesolimbic region of the brain selectively is sulpiride. The theoretical basis for the use of such medications is to affect the subpopulation of dopaminergic receptors that are believed most relevant to the pathophysiology of psychosis. Purported advantages of sulpiride include increased efficacy and reduced risk of tardive dyskinesia.

Pharmacotherapy in a Psychotherapeutic Context

Clinicians can improve treatment by paying attention to the role of pharmacotherapy within the broader treatment context. A patient's feelings and beliefs about taking medication are appropriate issues for discussion in individual and group psychotherapy sessions. When all involved pay attention to patients' concerns about medications' effects and side effects, the result is an improved pharmacotherapeutic alliance (Gutheil and Havens 1979).

This alliance is also enhanced by viewing the patient as an active collaborator rather than as a passive recipient of treatment. Medication compliance can be promoted by attending to individual patients' difficulties in forming a collaborative treatment relationship. Factors such as complexity of treatment regimen, fatalistic attitude, or cognitive disorganization can be addressed by specific maneuvers individualized to a patient's needs (Corrigan et al. 1990). This stance moves the clinician from "working on to working with the psychotic person" (Havens 1968, p. 49), allowing patients the chance to participate in the management of their own drug treatment, which can be an important step in their growth (Havens 1963). Patients may need encouragement to voice their concerns about medication and make clinicians aware of adverse medication effects. One consumer advocate (Blaska 1990) has eloquently catalogued some pitfalls of pharmacotherapy that patients can learn to recognize.

Conclusions

Our knowledge of the psychopharmacology of schizophrenia, after more than three decades, still centers on the utility of neuroleptic medication in reversing and preventing flagrant psychotic symptomatology. Yet only a portion of the long-term morbidity of this disorder derives from acute positive psychotic symptoms.

The cornerstones of managing the so-called negative symptoms of schizophrenia are to employ the smallest necessary dose of neuroleptic medication during maintenance treatment and to take whatever steps are necessary (such as the vigorous use of antiparkinsonian and other adjunctive medications) to counteract the neuroleptic's adverse effects. Adjunctive medications may play another role as well: antidepressants, benzodiazepines, lithium, and (more speculatively) dopamine agonists or stimulants may enhance the effectiveness of neuroleptics. We still have much to learn about how these might best be used and with which patients. More trials and studies need to be conducted that emphasize the specific phases of the disorder. Through such studies, new agents will be added to our armamentarium.

A conceptual corner has now been turned in this work. No longer do we regard mere symptom suppression as our aim. We must now consider stimulation of function to be of equal importance.

References

Adams P: Neuropsychiatric evaluation and treatment of delirium in the critically ill cancer patient. Cancer Bulletin 36:156–160, 1984

Adler L, Angrist B, Peselow E, et al: Efficacy of propranolol in neuroleptic-induced akathisia. J Clin Psychopharmacol 5:164–166, 1985

Adler L, Angrist B, Peselow E, et al: A controlled assessment of propranolol in the treatment of neuroleptic-induced akathisia. Br J Psychiatry 149:42–45, 1986

Andreasen NC, Olsen S: Negative vs. positive schizophrenia: definition and validation. Arch Gen Psychiatry 39:789–794, 1982

Andrews P, Hall JN, Snaith PR: A controlled trial of phenothiazine withdrawal in chronic schizophrenic patients. Br J Psychiatry 128:451–455, 1976

Baldessarini R: Chemotherapy in Psychiatry. Cambridge, MA, Harvard University Press, 1985

Barnes TRE, Braude WM: Akathisia variants and tardive dyskinesia. Arch Gen Psychiatry 42:874–878, 1985

Bartels SJ, Drake RE: Depressive symptoms in schizophrenia: comprehensive differential diagnosis. Compr Psychiatry 29:467–483, 1988

Bartko G, Herczeg I, Lador G: Clinical symptomatology and drug compliance in schizophrenic patients. Acta Psychiatr Scand 77:74–76, 1988

Becker RE: Implications of the efficacy of thiothixene and a chlorpromazine-imipramine combination for depression in schizophrenia. Am J Psychiatry 140:208–211, 1983

Berlant JL: Neuroleptics and reserpine in refractory psychoses. J Clin Psychopharmacol 6:180–184, 1986

Berlant JL: One more look at propranolol for the treatment of refractory schizophrenia. Schizophr Bull 13:705–714, 1987

Blaska B: The myriad medication mistakes in psychiatry: a consumer's view. Hosp Community Psychiatry 41:993–998, 1990

Boyer WF, Bakalar NH, Lake CR: Anticholinergic prophylaxis of acute haloperidol-induced acute dystonic reactions. J Clin Psychopharmacol 7:164–166, 1987

Braude WM, Barnes TRE, Gore SM: Clinical characteristics of akathisia: a systematic investigation of acute psychiatric inpatient admissions. Br J Psychiatry 143:139–150, 1983

Carpenter WT Jr, Heinrichs DW, Alphs LD: Treatment of negative symptoms. Schizophr Bull 11:440–452, 1985

Carpenter WT Jr, Heinrichs DW, Wagman AMI: Deficit and nondeficit forms of schizophrenia: the concept. Am J Psychiatry 145:578–583, 1988

Corrigan PW, Liberman RP, Engel JD: From noncompliance to collaboration in the treatment of schizophrenia. Hosp Community Psychiatry 41:1203–1211, 1990

Crow TJ: Molecular pathology of schizophrenia: more than one disease process? BMJ 280:66–68, 1980

Csernansky JG, Lombrozo L, Gulevich GO, et al: Treatment of negative schizophrenic symptoms with alprazolam: a preliminary open-label study. J Clin Psychopharmacol 4:349–352, 1984

Csernansky JG, Riney SJ, Lombrozo L, et al: Double-blind comparison of alprazolam, diazepam, and placebo for the treatment of negative schizophrenic symptoms. Arch Gen Psychiatry 45:655–659, 1988

Cutler NR, Jeste DV, Kaufmann CA, et al: Low-dose bromocriptine: a study of acute effects in chronic medicated schizophrenics. Prog Neuropsychopharmacol Biol Psychiatry 8:277–283, 1984

Davis JM: Maintenance therapy and the natural course of schizophrenia. J Clin Psychiatry 11(suppl):18–21, 1985a

Davis JM: Overview: Maintenance therapy in psychiatry, I: schizophrenia. Am J Psychiatry 132:1237–1245, 1985b

Davis JM, Andriukaitis S: The natural course of schizophrenia and effective maintenance drug treatment. J Clin Psychopharmacol 6:2S–10S, 1986

Dixon D: Respiratory depression following midazolam (letter). Anaesthesia 40:922, 1985

Donaldson SR, Gelenberg AJ, Baldessarini J: The pharmacologic treatment of schizophrenia: a progress report. Schizophr Bull 9:504–527, 1983

Dose M, Apelt S, Emrich HM: Carbamazepine as an adjunct of antipsychotic therapy. Psychiatry Res 22:303–310, 1987

Drake RE, Osher FC, Wallach MA: Alcohol use and abuse in schizophrenia: a prospective community study. J Nerv Ment Dis 177:408–414, 1989

Dubin WR, Weiss KJ, Dorn JM: Pharmacotherapy of psychiatric emergencies. J Clin Psychopharmacol 6:210–222, 1986

Dworkin RJ, Adams GL: Pharmacotherapy of the chronic patient: gender and diagnostic factors. Community Ment Health J 20:253–261, 1984

Eckman TA, Liberman RP, Phipps CC, et al: Teaching medication management skills to schizophrenia patients. J Clin Psychopharmacol 10:33–38, 1990

Ellison JM, Jacobs D: Emergency psychopharmacology: a review and update. Ann Emerg Med 15:962–968, 1986

Escobar JI, Barron A, Kiriakos R: A controlled study of neuroleptization with fluphenazine hydrochloride injections. J Clin Psychopharmacol 3:359–362, 1983

Fleishhacker WW, Roth SD, Kane JM: The pharmacologic treatment of neuroleptic-induced akathisia. J Clin Psychopharmacol 10:12–21, 1990

Gelenberg AJ: Treating extrapyramidal reactions: some current issues. J Clin Psychiatry 48(9 suppl):24–27, 1987

Gutheil TG, Havens LL: The therapeutic alliance: contemporary meanings and confusions. Reviews in Psychoanalysis 6:467–481, 1979

Havens LL: Problems with the use of drugs in the psychotherapy of psychotic patients. Psychiatry 26:289–296, 1963

Havens LL: Some difficulties in giving schizophrenic and borderline patients medication. Psychiatry 31:44–50, 1968

Herz MI, Melville C: Relapse in schizophrenia. Am J Psychiatry 137:801–805, 1980

Hogarty GE: Depot neuroleptics: the relevance of psychosocial factors. J Clin Psychiatry 45(suppl):36 42, 1984

Hogarty GE, Goldberg SC: Collaborative Study Group: drug and sociotherapy in the aftercare of schizophrenic patients. Arch Gen Psychiatry 28:54–64, 1973

Hogarty GE, Goldberg SC, Schooler NR, et al: Drug and sociotherapy in the aftercare of schizophrenic patients, II: two-year relapse rates. Arch Gen Psychiatry 31:603–608, 1974

Johnson DAW: Studies of depressive symptoms in schizophrenia. Br J Psychiatry 139:89–101, 1981

Kahn JP, Puertollano MA, Schane MD, et al: Adjunctive alprazolam for schizophrenia with panic anxiety: clinical observation and pathogenetic implications. Am J Psychiatry 145:742–744, 1988

Kane JM: Compliance issues in outpatient treatment. J Clin Psychopharmacol 5:22S–27S, 1985
Kane JM: Treatment of schizophrenia. Schizophr Bull 13:133–156, 1987
Kane JM, Rifkin A, Woerner M, et al: Low-dose neuroleptic treatment of outpatient schizophrenics, I: preliminary results for relapse rates. Arch Gen Psychiatry 40:893–896, 1983
Kellner R, Wilson RM, Muldawer MD, et al: Anxiety in schizophrenia: the responses to chlordiazepoxide in an intensive design study. Arch Gen Psychiatry 32:1246–1254, 1975
Kirkpatrick B, Burnett GB: Observations on neuroleptic use in acutely psychotic patients. J Clin Psychopharmacol 2:205–207, 1982
Klein DF, Gittelman R, Quitkin F, et al: Diagnosis and Drug Treatment of Psychiatric Disorders: Adults and Children, 2nd Edition. Baltimore, MD, Williams & Wilkins, 1980
Knights A, Hirsch SR: "Revealed" depression and drug treatment for schizophrenia. Arch Gen Psychiatry 38:806–811, 1981
Kolakowska T, Williams AO, Ardern M, et al: Schizophrenia with good and poor outcome, I: early clinical features, response to neuroleptics and signs of organic dysfunction. Br J Psychiatry 146:229–246, 1985
Levi-Minzi S, Bermanzohn PC, Siris SG: Bromocriptine for negative symptoms in schizophrenia. Compr Psychiatry (in press)
Lieberman JA, Kane JM, Sarantakos S, et al: Prediction of relapse in schizophrenia. Arch Gen Psychiatry 44:597–603, 1986
Lipinski JF Jr, Zubenko GS, Cohen BM, et al: Propranolol in the treatment of neuroleptic-induced akathisia. Am J Psychiatry 141:412–415, 1984
Ludatscher JI: Stable remission of tardive dyskinesia by L-dopa. J Clin Psychopharmacol 9:39–41, 1989
McGlashan TH, Carpenter WT Jr: Postpsychotic depression in schizophrenia. Arch Gen Psychiatry 33:231–241, 1976
Mandel MR, Severe JB, Schooler NR, et al: Development and prediction of post-psychotic depression in neuroleptic-treated schizophrenics. Arch Gen Psychiatry 39:197–203, 1982
Marder SR, Van Putten T: Who should receive clozapine? Arch Gen Psychiatry 45:865–867, 1988
Marder SR, Van Putten T, Mintz J, et al: Low- and conventional-dose maintenance therapy with fluphenazine decanoate: two-year outcome. Arch Gen Psychiatry 44:518–521, 1987
Martin RL, Cloninger CR, Guze SB, et al: Frequency and differential diagnosis of depressive syndromes in schizophrenia. J Clin Psychiatry 46(11, Sec 2):9–13, 1985
Mason AS, Forrest IS, Forrest FW, et al: Adherence to maintenance therapy and rehospitalization. Diseases of the Nervous System 24:103–104, 1963

Meltzer HY: Dopamine and negative symptoms in schizophrenia: critique of the type I-II hypotheses, in Controversies in Schizophrenia. Edited by Alpert M. New York, Guilford, 1985

Meltzer HY, Stahl S: The dopamine hypothesis: a review. Schizophr Bull 2:19–76, 1976

Meltzer HY, Sommers AA, Luchins DJ: The effect of neuroleptics and other psychotropic drugs on negative symptoms in schizophrenia. J Clin Psychopharmacol 6:329–338, 1986

Mendoza R, Djenderedjian AH, Adams J, et al: Midazolam in acute psychotic patients with hyperarousal. J Clin Psychiatry 48:291–292, 1987

Neborsky R, Janowsky D, Munson E, et al: Rapid treatment of acute psychotic symptoms with high- and low-dose haloperidol. Arch Gen Psychiatry 38:195–199, 1987

Osser DN: Treatment-resistant problems, in Handbook of Clinical Psychopharmacology, 2nd Edition. Edited by Tupin JP, Shader RI, Harnett DS. New York, Jason Aronson, 1988

Pelonero AL, Elliott RL: Ethical and clinical considerations in selecting patients who will receive clozapine. Hosp Community Psychiatry 41:878–880, 1990

Pogue-Geile MF, Zubin J: Negative symptomatology and schizophrenia: a conceptual and empirical review. International Journal of Mental Health 16:3–45, 1988

Prien RF, Levine J, Switalski RW: Discontinuation of chemotherapy for chronic schizophrenia. Hosp Community Psychiatry 2:20–23, 1971

Prusoff BA, Williams DH, Weissman MM, et al: Treatment of secondary depression in schizophrenia. Arch Gen Psychiatry 36:569–575, 1979

Rifkin A, Quitkin F, Klein DF: Akinesia: a poorly recognized drug-induced extrapyramidal behavioral disorder. Arch Gen Psychiatry 32:672–674, 1975

Salzman C, Green AI, Rodriguez-Villa F, et al: Benzodiazepines combined with neuroleptics for management of severe disruptive behavior. Psychosomatics 27(suppl):17–21, 1986

Sandberg L, Siris SG: "Panic disorder" in schizophrenia: a case report. J Nerv Ment Dis 175:627–628, 1987

Schaffer CB, Shahid A, Javaid JI, et al: Bioavailability of intramuscular versus oral haloperidol in schizophrenic patients. J Clin Psychopharmacol 2:274–277, 1982

Seeman MV: Gender differences in schizophrenia. Can J Psychiatry 27:107–112, 1982

Seeman MV: Interaction of sex, age, and neuroleptic dose. Compr Psychiatry 24:125–128, 1983

Singh AN, Saxena B, Nelson HL: A controlled clinical study of trazodone in chronic schizophrenic patients with pronounced depressive symptomatology. Current Therapeutic Research 23:485–501, 1978

Siris SG: Akathisia and "acting out." J Clin Psychiatry 47:86–88, 1985

Siris SG: Akinesia and postpsychotic depression: a difficult differential diagnosis. J Clin Psychiatry 48:240–243, 1987

Siris SG: Pharmacological treatment of depression in schizophrenia, in Depression and Schizophrenia. Edited by DeLisi L. Washington, DC, American Psychiatric Association (in press)

Siris SG, van Kammen DP, Docherty JP: Use of antidepressant drugs in schizophrenia. Arch Gen Psychiatry 35:1368–1377, 1978

Siris SG, Harmon GK, Endicott J: Postpsychotic depressive symptoms in hospitalized schizophrenic patients. Arch Gen Psychiatry 38:1122–1123, 1981

Siris SG, Morgan V, Fagerstrom R, et al: Adjunctive imipramine in the treatment of postpsychotic depression: a controlled trial. Arch Gen Psychiatry 35:1368–1377, 1987

Siris SG, Adan F, Cohen M, et al: Postpsychotic depression and vegetative symptoms: an investigation of syndromal overlap. Am J Psychiatry 145:1532–1537, 1988

Siris SG, Aronson A, Sellew AP: Imipramine-responsive paniclike symptomatology in schizophrenia. Biol Psychiatry 25:485–488, 1989

Sommers AA: Negative symptoms: conceptual and methodological problems. Schizophr Bull 11:364–377, 1985

Stahl SM: Akathisia and tardive dyskinesia: changing concepts. Arch Gen Psychiatry 42:915–917, 1985

Strang JS, Falloon IR, Moss HB, et al: Effects of family therapy on treatment compliance in schizophrenia. Psychopharmacol Bull 17:87–88, 1981

Tamminga CA, Gerlach J: New neuroleptics and experimental antipsychotics in schizophrenia, in Psychopharmacology: The Third Generation of Progress. Edited by Meltzer HY. New York, Raven, 1987

Tesar GE, Murray GB, Cassem NH: Use of high-dose intravenous haloperidol in the treatment of agitated cardiac patients. J Clin Psychopharmacol 5:344–347, 1985

Tune L, Coyle JY: Serum levels of anticholinergic drugs in treatment of acute extrapyramidal side effects. Arch Gen Psychiatry 37:293–297, 1990

Van Putten T: Why do schizophrenic patients refuse to take their drugs? Arch Gen Psychiatry 31:67–72, 1974

Van Putten T: The many faces of akathisia. Compr Psychiatry 16:43–47, 1975

Van Putten T, May PRA: Subjective response as a predictor of outcome in pharmacotherapy: the consumer has a point. Arch Gen Psychiatry 35:477–488, 1978a

Van Putten T, May PRA: "Akinetic depression" in schizophrenia. Arch Gen Psychiatry 35:1101–1107, 1978b

Van Putten T, May PRA, Marder SR: Akathisia with haloperidol and thiothixene. Arch Gen Psychiatry 41:1036–1039, 1984

Vaughn CE, Snyder KS, Jones S, et al: Family factors in schizophrenic relapse. Arch Gen Psychiatry 41:1169–1177, 1984

Waehrens J, Gerlach J: Antidepressant drugs in anergic schizophrenia: a double-blind crossover study with maprotiline and placebo. Acta Psychiatr Scand 61:438–444, 1980

Walker E, Lewine RJ: The positive/negative symptom distinction in schizophrenia: validity and etiological relevance. Schizophrenia Research 1:315–328, 1988

Woerner MG, Kane JM, Lieberman JA, et al: The prevalence of tardive dyskinesia. J Clin Psychopharmacol 11:34–53, 1991

Wolkowitz OM, Pickar D, Doran AR, et al: Combination alprazolam-neuroleptic treatment of the positive and negative symptoms of schizophrenia. Am J Psychiatry 143:85–87, 1986

Wolkowitz OM, Breier A, Doran A, et al: Alprazolam augmentation of the antipsychotic effects of fluphenazine in schizophrenic patients: preliminary results. Arch Gen Psychiatry 45:664–671, 1988

Young JL, Zanona HV, Shepler L: Medication noncompliance in schizophrenia: codification and update. Bull Am Acad Psychiatry Law 14:105–122, 1986

Young MA, Meltzer HY: The relationship of demographic, clinical, and outcome variables to neuroleptic treatment requirements. Schizophr Bull 6:88–101, 1980

5

Implications for Psychosocial Interventions in Patients With Schizophrenia

Historically, psychosocial interventions have been the mainstay of the psychiatric care of people with schizophrenia. The advent of effective psychotropic drugs both stimulated interest in redefining the role of psychosocial interventions and made patients more amenable to such interventions. Many people with schizophrenia continue to struggle with persistent and severe social and vocational impairments despite the ameliorative effects of psychotropic medications on disruptive symptoms. Recent evidence suggests that psychosocial interventions do have an effect and that this effect is important. In order to go beyond symptom suppression, we now need to refine our understanding of these treatment techniques and of their integration into the longitudinal care of individuals with schizophrenia.

This chapter presents an overview of studies of psychosocial interventions in schizophrenia, proceeding from the most narrow type of intervention (individual psychotherapy) to the broadest longitudinal care approaches currently available (continuous treatment teams). The review is not exhaustive. The literature on individual, group, and family psychotherapeutic interventions is probably familiar to most mental health professionals. We will summarize these interventions briefly and devote more discussion to the newer and less familiar models of psychosocial rehabilitation. The reader is referred to the extensive bibliography for more detailed information.

This review indicates where additional research is needed in order to determine how the longitudinal care approach can be enhanced through effective psychosocial interventions. At the core of this approach lies the need to create a supportive environment in which the individual with schizophrenia can function and develop. Ultimately, longitudinal care may help these patients find meaning in their lives and help relieve the perplexity so common and painful in them.

Psychotherapy

Individual Psychotherapy

Since 1960, six controlled clinical trials of individual psychotherapy with schizophrenic patients have been carried out (Fairweather and Sanders 1969; Fairweather et al. 1960; Grinspoon et al. 1972; Gunderson et al. 1984; Karon and VandenBos 1981; May 1968; Rogers et al. 1967; Stanton et al. 1984). Their results have raised the question of whether intensive, individual psychotherapy is justified in either the acute or chronic phases of the illness.

Although they did not provide evidence of clear efficacy of one psychotherapeutic treatment over another, these studies have led to several important conclusions regarding psychotherapy and schizophrenia:

1. The treatment of schizophrenia is a complex undertaking requiring multiple specific interventions, applied to patients in an appropriate sequence depending on their phase of the illness.
2. A supportive therapeutic relationship with a trained professional may result in significant improvements in social functioning and major role performance. Further, the recent findings of Frank and Gunderson (1990) have demonstrated the importance of the therapeutic alliance on medication compliance and treatment continuation.
3. Psychotherapy and pharmacotherapy are clinically compatible, and the studies provide some guidelines for integration of divergent treatment techniques to achieve stress reduction, to enhance coping skills in patients and their families, and to reduce relapse rates.
4. Pharmacological treatment is less independent of psychosocial factors than was previously thought.
5. New research strategies are needed to capture the complexity and dynamic quality of the disease process in schizophrenia.

Together with recent long-term, naturalistic studies of the treatment and recovery process (Docherty et al. 1978; Harding et al. 1987; Strauss et al. 1981), these controlled-outcome studies have set the stage for the next generation of research on the individual psychotherapy of patients with schizophrenia.

Group Psychotherapy

Group psychotherapy has long been part of the armamentarium of therapeutic interventions with people diagnosed as schizophrenic. Although dozens of reports and controlled studies have examined the use of group psychotherapy with these individuals (Bednar and Lawlis 1971; Erikson 1982; Kanas 1986; May and Simpson 1980; Mosher and Keith 1980; O'Brien 1975; Parloff and Dies 1977; Scott and Griffith 1982; Stotsky and Zolik 1965; Yalom 1983), its role remains controversial. The many methodological inconsistencies in these studies—including varying inclusion criteria, diagnostic heterogeneity, inappropriate control groups, and unspecified or poorly described medication status, therapeutic methods, and duration of treatment and follow-up, as well as the lack of application of meta-analytic statistical techniques—make it difficult to reach clear conclusions. Furthermore, the widespread use of group settings in the delivery of many psychosocial interventions has challenged our definition of what constitutes group psychotherapy.

Nevertheless, several statements can be made about group psychotherapy for patients with schizophrenia:

1. The positive therapeutic experience of joining a group can be of central importance in rehabilitation of individuals with disturbed ego boundaries and marked social dysfunction (Stone 1990).
2. The promotion of socialization and enhanced interpersonal skills is a more likely outcome of group psychotherapy than is an effect on rehospitalization, psychopathology, or work performance.
3. Principles derived from our understanding of family dynamics, especially the beneficial effect of decreasing hostility in the schizophrenic patient's environment, may be applicable in the group therapy setting as well (Kanas et al. 1989). (These principles are discussed in the next section.)
4. Many of the principles of traditional psychoanalytically oriented group psychotherapy cannot be as helpfully applied to individuals with schizophrenia. Groups for people with schizophrenia require different techniques, such as the noninterpretation of metaphors, individualized attendance contracts, a relaxed prohibition on contact with group members outside of the session, and a decreased use of confrontation.

5. Finally, the literature clearly demonstrates the need for further research that uses modern methodology and large samples in order to investigate group therapy further. Specifically, this research will need to examine the parameters of type of treatment, duration, setting, interaction with other psychosocial and pharmacological treatments, and subtypes of patients who might respond optimally to various forms of treatment. It is also not clear what specific therapeutic ingredients of group therapy account for the effectiveness and widespread use of group approaches to rehabilitation, medication, and psychoeducation.

Family Interventions

As the individual with schizophrenia strives to progress during adult development, a stable and supportive environment is crucial. Because many people with schizophrenia now live with their families in the community, a great deal of research on social supports over the past 30 years has focused on the family (Group for the Advancement of Psychiatry 1985). In fact, the recognition that family attitudes and behaviors can markedly affect relapse rates and social adaptation is perhaps the most exciting development in the psychosocial treatment of schizophrenia today.

Studies of the familial environment (Brown et al. 1958, 1972; Leff et al. 1982; Vaughn and Leff 1976; Vaughn et al. 1984) have enhanced our understanding of the complex interaction between and among the individual, the illness, and the environment. Several investigators (Anderson et al. 1980; Falloon et al. 1982, 1985; Goldstein et al. 1978; Hogarty et al. 1986, 1988; Leff et al. 1982) have shown that helping families to increase their knowledge of mental illness, their communication and coping skills, and their social supports can significantly reduce the risk of relapse for their schizophrenic relatives.

Family intervention strategies differ primarily along format parameters such as the setting (clinic, hospital, or home), orientation (crisis versus maintenance), number of sessions, and membership (inclusion or exclusion of the patient in the sessions, and single versus multiple family approaches). Although the specifics vary, each approach involves the enlistment of the family in a positive clinical alliance, the provision of psychoeducational material about the nature of schizophrenia and about techniques for improved communication and problem solving, and the encouragement of families to expand their social networks through mutual interest and self-help groups, such as the National Alliance for the Mentally Ill (NAMI).

Family members are taught how to cope with aberrations in the schizophrenic patient's behavior. In some psychoeducational treatment approaches, an effort is made to maintain essential family boundaries, to clarify family roles, and to progressively increase the social role competence of the patient. Recent work has shown that even more dramatic improvements can be obtained by combining this approach with social skills training for the patient (Hogarty et al. 1986), with training in the recognition of early signs of decompensation (Herz and Melville 1980), and even with enlisting family members in performing important case management functions such as assessment, monitoring, crisis intervention, and advocacy (Intagliata et al. 1986).

Much of the work on familial environment has been done in relation to the expressed emotion (EE) construct, which has come to refer primarily to the degree of hostile and critical interactions in the environment (Leff et al. 1982; Vaughn and Leff 1976; Vaughn et al. 1984). The EE construct is controversial for several reasons. Parker and colleagues (1988) have been unable to demonstrate a correlation between EE and relapse. The work of MacMillan and others (1986) similarly casts doubt on the validity of EE as a predictor of outcome or medication response. Kanter and colleagues (1987), in their critical review of the EE construct, question the causal relationship between EE and relapse and describe many methodological limitations in the EE literature. Furthermore, the EE construct has rekindled fears of blaming families for their relatives' illness, much as the "schizophrenogenic family" construct used to do (Fromm-Reichmann 1948; Strachan 1986).

The EE construct is not necessary to validate the importance of the new family interventions. Their effectiveness can be explained equally well in terms of providing families with what they report they need (Bernheim and Lehman 1985; Lefley 1987). Similar interventions have been developed for families with relatives who have other impairments such as dementia (Smyer and Birkel 1989). To the extent that hostile and critical communications are harmful for people with schizophrenia, the concept applies to nonfamilial environments as well. Developments in group, milieu, and inpatient treatments, as well as interventions for nonfamilial living environments, reflect adherence to the principle of creating nonhostile, noncritical environments of benign support. This is especially important during the early stages of psychotic decompensation and reintegration (Carpenter et al. 1988).

Rehabilitation

In the last few decades, we have witnessed substantive advances in our understanding of the schizophrenic individual's functional impairments and need for rehabilitative interventions that are aimed at minimizing social and occupational handicaps and maximizing community adjustment. Furthermore, we more clearly understand the need for habilitation as well as rehabilitation—that is, the need to redress the fundamental deficits created by the developmental disruption associated with the intrusion of florid psychoses into young lives. There can no longer be any doubt that inactivity leads to additional disabilities not inherent in the underlying illness (Mechanic 1986). The need, therefore, to engage patients in rehabilitative treatment should be obvious. Moreover, they should be involved actively in planning their rehabilitation interventions.

A thorough assessment of the individual's strengths, deficits, needs, and desires is crucial. Although little empirical evidence exists to support conclusively the need for any given assessment method, the following models are mentioned in the literature as useful.

The highly structured skills training programs of UCLA/Brentwood Veterans' Administration Hospital (Kuehnel and Liberman 1988; Liberman et al. 1985; Wallace 1986) and Boston University (Anthony 1980) use a detailed behavioral or functional assessment to identify specific skills deficits—receiving, processing, and sending skills—as defined by the individual's current skills level, and that range of skills necessary to succeed in the person's living environment. Assertive Community Treatment (ACT) programs (Stein and Test 1985) emphasize community-based assessments, whereas psychosocial rehabilitation (PSR) centers (Beard et al. 1982; Glasscote 1971) use prevocational work crews as a context for assessment. Assessments of psychiatric symptoms (Lukoff et al. 1986a) and of neuropsychological deficits (Carpenter et al. 1988; Spaulding et al. 1986) may also be important tools in the formulation and ongoing evaluation of an individualized rehabilitative treatment plan. Finally, there is a growing appreciation that the patients' subjective experience of their illness, along with their goals, ambitions, and hunger for normalcy, is of critical importance in all phases of assessment and treatment (Strauss 1989).

There is also a growing awareness of gender differences in approaches to vocational rehabilitation. Specifically, female role stereotypes that minimize the value of paid work for women lead to narrowed expectations for the chronically ill woman with schizophrenia (Bachrach 1985; Carmen et al. 1981; Zeldow 1978). Goering and colleagues (1984; Wasylenki et al. 1985) have reported that not only are women with chronic schizophrenia as interested in active employment as similarly diagnosed men but they also are apparently more acceptable in the work force. These results highlight the dependence of women's vocational success on different factors—such as assertiveness training and specialized support systems (child care, transportation, and homemaking)—than those factors important in men. Future rehabilitation programs must incorporate these changes to help women be successful.

There are a wide variety and diversity of rehabilitation programs, differing in philosophy, structure, setting, and cost. We will provide an overview here of the major models in practice, as well as discuss the strengths and limitations of each based on current empirical knowledge (see Table 5–1 for a summary of these models).

The Psychosocial Rehabilitation Center

The Psychosocial Rehabilitation (PSR) Center, as exemplified by Fountain House in New York (Beard et al. 1982; Glasscote 1971), is based on the concept of self-help and de-emphasis of the patient role. Activities include social rehabilitation within an informal "clubhouse" setting; problem-solving groups; assistance with basic living needs, such as housing, food, clothing, and medical needs; and vocational services, ranging from prevocational work crews to transitional employment (TE) in which the client is placed into a job in the community that is contracted by the PSR Center. The PSR model has been widely disseminated and is fairly generalizable (Stratoudakis 1986).

Outcome studies have focused on rehospitalization and vocational placement. In an uncontrolled study, Beard and colleagues (1978) demonstrated significantly lower rehospitalization rates at 1, 2, and 5 years for individuals at Fountain House who received "reaching-out" techniques to enhance their participation in the rehabilitation program. The vocational outcome data reveal a difficult transition to competitive employment, with as few as 5% of clients functioning in competitive employment in a Maryland study of 28 PSRs (Conners et al. 1987). There has been no systematic evaluation of the effectiveness of PSRs in terms of overall social adjustment.

Second-Generation PSR Programs

Evolving from the PSR model have been programs such as Thresholds in Chicago (Bond, in press; Bond et al. 1984; Dincin 1975). These programs include some of the previously discussed tools, as well as residential facilities and, as in the case of the Thresholds' Bridge Program (Witheridge 1985), an integration of assertive community treatment (discussed in the next section). These programs have incorporated the use of a "job bank" vocational concept, which (as with transitional

Table 5–1. Models of psychosocial rehabilitation

Model	Summary
Psychosocial Rehabilitation (PSR) Center *Example:* Fountain House	Client-centered "clubhouse" with self-help and de-emphasis of the patient role Prevocational work crews and transitional employment (TE) Assistance with basic living needs Plus/minus outreach
Second-Generation PSR Programs *Example:* Thresholds	Job bank Assertive outreach Community Scholars Program
Assertive Community Treatment (ACT) *Example:* PACT	Assertive case management with centralized responsibility Emphasis on flexible, highly individualized care 24-hour-a-day availability Family and community support
Boston University (BU) Model	Client-centered skills training approach "Choose-get-keep" vocational approach with extensive prevocational training Emphasis on client's choices Training program for rehabilitation professionals
Social Skills Training (SST) Program *Example:* UCLA/Brentwood VA	Highly programmed social skills training based on learning theory Utilization of role-play, peer support, and rewarding environment Job club Videotapes and manuals allow for dissemination
Supported Employment (SE)	Competitive employment in integrated setting with ongoing support Time unlimited

employment) relies on a relationship between the agency and cooperating employers but offers a greater diversity of settings and schedules, allowing the clients greater flexibility to suit their abilities, ambitions, and needs. Thresholds also developed the Community Scholars Program in which the client is assisted in completing a high school equivalency degree or course work at a university or technical school. As with Fountain House, Thresholds demonstrated a significant effect on reducing rehospitalization rates (Dincin and Witheridge 1982) although, interestingly, this was seen only among male subjects. There are no published evaluations of the occupational or social outcomes of this form of treatment.

Assertive Community Treatment

Assertive Community Treatment (ACT) is based on the Training in Community Living (TCL) model developed in the early 1970s at Mendota Mental Health Institute in Madison, Wisconsin (Marx et al. 1973). This consists of assertive community-based care founded on a team case management model, capitalizing on patients' strengths and providing support as needed on a 24-hour-a-day basis. An emphasis is placed on flexible and highly individualized comprehensive treatment delivered in an ongoing time-unlimited manner aimed at preventing and limiting chronic functional impairment (Stein and Test 1985; Test 1979; Test et al. 1985). Community and family support and education are provided as well, and resources are enlisted within the community to support the rehabilitation activities. Although this model is best represented in the Program for Assertive Community Treatment (PACT) in Madison, Wisconsin, it has been adopted in a number of other communities throughout the United States and overseas, as in Sydney, Australia.

Experimental data gathered in many communities demonstrate the efficacy of ACT in reducing the number and length of hospitalizations (Bond et al. 1988; Borland et al. 1989; Hoult et al. 1983; Mulder 1982; Stein and Test 1980; Wright et al. 1989). However, as Olfson (1990) has pointed out in his review of ACT, this does not necessarily imply a reduction in the level of psychopathology, enhanced social or vocational functioning, an increased sense of patient or family well-being, or an improvement in public safety. Existing experimental evidence tends to demonstrate that ACT is at least as effective as traditional treatment in these areas, but there is clearly the need for controlled longitudinal studies in which subjects are randomized to ACT versus conventional community care—such as that currently being conducted by Test in Madison—in order to address these issues adequately. Research is also needed to identify those patients who will respond optimally to ACT versus other forms of treatment, to define the "active ingredients" of ACT, and to clarify the overall cost-effectiveness of ACT. In addition, future research should utilize state-of-the-art comparison groups, evaluate mature established ACT programs, and have follow-up periods of 18 months or more (Taube et al. 1990).

The Boston University Model

The Boston University (BU) model (Anthony 1980; Anthony and Blanch 1989; Farkas and Anthony 1989) places a combined emphasis on skills training and client-centered approaches. It is predominantly center-based and involves an extensive evaluation of the patient's skills, with subsequent training of identified deficits. An important feature is the model's focus on the patient's choice in both living and vocational environments.

The skills level needed to succeed in the chosen settings is the targeted rehabilitation endpoint. Although training is center-based, efforts are made to enhance the generalizability of the learned skills into the community, in part by enlisting the natural caregivers in the skills training process. Vocational rehabilitation is based on a "choose-get-keep" concept (Danley and Rogers 1988) and consists of a three-step process, with extensive prevocational work adjustment training and career counseling phases, followed by career placement. The BU model has a training program for rehabilitation professionals (Rogers et al. 1986), and the model has been disseminated into many communities.

By and large, there has been little experimental validation of the BU model. Goering and colleagues (1988) followed 82 patients (experimental treatment versus historically matched controls) for 2 years; the experimental subjects were treated by case managers trained in the BU model. No significant difference in the rate of paid employment was demonstrated, although a significant difference favoring the experimental treatment was demonstrated on a measure of "instrumental role" (a broadened definition of occupational functioning including such roles as student, homemaker, and volunteer, as well as paid worker). There is certainly a need for further experimental evaluation of this model before its efficacy can be considered established.

The Social Skills Training Program

The Social Skills Training (SST) Program of UCLA/Brentwood Veterans' Administration (VA) Hospital (Liberman 1982a, 1988; Liberman et al.

1985, 1986) is based on learning theory and the "stress-vulnerability-coping-competence" model of chronic mental illness (Liberman 1982b). This program uses behavioral techniques to teach even the most chronic patients symptom self-management and instrumental and affiliative skills. This treatment approach, which can be applied in individual, family, or group settings, relies on a identification of patient skills and deficits, as well as on environmental supports and demands, with subsequent skills training using role-playing, peer support, and a rewarding environment.

This technique has been used to train skills pertaining to basic communication, recreation and leisure, friendship and dating, medication self-management (Liberman et al. 1989), vocational rehabilitation (Jacobs 1988), and sexual behavior (Lukoff et al. 1986b). The vocational rehabilitation component of the program uses a spectrum of services, including the "job club" (Azrin and Phillip 1979), which involves a time-limited job-finding skills training program followed by a full-time job search. Dissemination of the UCLA model has been facilitated by its condensation into treatment manuals (Liberman et al. 1989) and a series of videotape training modules.

Three published controlled trials have looked at the efficacy of social skills training in schizophrenic patients. Bellack and colleagues (1984) found SST plus day treatment to be superior to day treatment alone along measures of social competence but not regarding rate of rehospitalization. Substantial sample attrition, especially among control subjects, may limit the generalizations that can be made from this study. Wallace and Liberman (1985) also found a significant improvement on measures of social competence and adjustment, but not rate of rehospitalization or anxiety, for subjects randomized to SST versus holistic health therapy, with both groups receiving family therapy and pharmacotherapy. However, this effect was more clearly demonstrated at 9 months than at 24 months, implying a difficulty in maintaining the effect. Hogarty and colleagues (1986) found a significant reduction in relapse rates for subjects treated with either SST or family treatment, as compared with those who had only traditional individual supportive therapy (all subjects having received pharmacotherapy), and an additive effect among those who received the combination of SST plus family treatment.

Employment outcome using the job club approach has been reported (Azrin and Phillip 1979; Eisenberg and Cole 1986; Jacobs 1988; Keith et al. 1977). These studies have described an impressive effect on job placement among a diagnostically heterogeneous study sample, but the effect becomes much less substantial when only individuals with schizophrenia are considered (Bond, in press).

Although the Social Skills Training model seems to offer promise, there are basic considerations that remain unclear. The specific nature of the social deficits found in this heterogeneous group of individuals is not yet clearly understood (Morrison and Bellack 1987), and the relationship between social skills and the course or outcome of schizophrenia is inconclusive (Liberman 1982a). Furthermore, Bellack and colleagues (1989) have questioned the premise that problem-solving behavior is trainable, and they caution that "claims for the validity of the model and effectiveness of the procedures should be tempered until their generalizability and range of applicability can be determined" (p. 113).

Supported Employment

Finally, let us consider the Supported Employment (SE) model described in detail by Bond (in press) in his extensive review of vocational rehabilitation. This model, first described by Wehman and Moon (1988) and developed for people with mental retardation, is now being applied to the mentally ill (Bond 1987). It consists of 1) competitive employment in 2) an integrated work setting with 3) the provision of ongoing support services. Although SE shares some similarities with transitional employment (TE), the critical difference is that TE is time-limited, whereas SE is not. The influence of this final factor on long-term job retention—a frequent criticism of practically all existing vocational rehabilitation models—remains to be seen.

Conclusions and Recommendations

Four major conclusions can be drawn from the current status of the fertile and exciting field of psychosocial interventions:

1. Many of these interventions have now demonstrated clear and useful *efficacy*, meeting acceptable scientific standards of clinical assessment. This represents an important step forward for this field, and it provides the basis for continued empirical work to establish the verifiable effectiveness of these treatments and programs.
2. Appropriate, technically skillful interventions should be available to patients for all aspects of the psychosocial substance of their lives. The structure of this chapter, which has covered individual and group therapy, family psychoeducational training, social and vocational skills training, specialized rehabilitation centers, and active community support services, reflects the contemporary

recognition of the need for a *full psychosocial system of care.* Such a system must help to create changes in the patient's ability to cope as well as changes in the environment, rendering it consistent with the patient's abilities.

3. The nature of the psychosocial intervention should be consistent with the patient's current competence. Specifically, anxiety-provoking, emotion-arousing, insight-oriented therapies tend to have negative consequences when used with individuals with schizophrenia in both the acute and the prolonged postacute phase of care. This is reflected in data from individual therapy, interactions in the family, and reactions to the demand pressures of certain social skills and vocational training programs. On the positive side, the recognition of the patients' often exquisite sensitivity and constraints on their autonomous therapeutic response has spawned the development of many new models for psychosocial care. It has led to the development of specific foci for improving the quality and efficacy of these interventions. These models include:

   a. *Sequencing:* The sequence in which interventions should be introduced into the patient's care is not well understood. What should come first? How long must one intervention be in place before another is begun? Another way of framing this question is to ask, what are the patient criteria, as well as what is the necessary psychobiological context, for optimizing the success and minimizing the failures of specific interventions?

   b. *Enhancing engagement:* It has become clear that more attention must be paid to effective methods and techniques for engaging patients in the available (and sometimes newly available) treatment interventions. Such ongoing efforts include, for example, the focus on dual diagnosis and the role of substance abuse in limiting therapeutic engagement and response.

   c. *The development of novel strategies:* The clarifying perception of the broad spectrum of deficits, difficulties, and special needs of people with schizophrenia has generated great interest in developing new creative methods of care. One promising development, for example, is neuropsychological assessment-based cognitive retraining, an effort to correct the fundamental limiting cognitive deficits of the individual with schizophrenia. In addition, there appears to be a developing iterative process that has potential benefits. For example, although the results of individual therapy have seemed limited, some current work suggests that individual therapy, timed appropriately and following a period of prolonged stabilization of symptoms and the social environment as well as skill building, may be incrementally beneficial.

4. Finally, the technology of psychosocial care currently being developed is still not widely known and practiced. Programs and resources need to be developed to support the effective *dissemination of this knowledge.*

The doors have opened on an era offering truly individualized and comprehensive psychosocial care for people with schizophrenia. As the interventions described in this chapter are applied, refined, augmented, and even replaced with future approaches, an opportunity exists for achieving social and vocational successes previously beyond the reach of those affected by schizophrenia.

References

Anderson CM, Hogarty GE, Reiss DJ: Family treatment of adult schizophrenic patients: a psychoeducational approach. Schizophr Bull 6(3):490–505, 1980

Anthony WA: The Principles of Psychiatric Rehabilitation. Baltimore, MD, University Park Press, 1980

Anthony WA, Blanch A: Research on community support services: what have we learned? Psychosocial Rehabilitation Journal 12:55–81, 1989

Azrin NH, Phillip RA: The job-club method for the job handicapped: a comparative outcome study. Rehabilitation Counseling Bulletin 23:144–155, 1979

Bachrach LL: Chronically mentally ill women: emergence and legitimation of program issues. Hosp Community Psychiatry 36:1063–1069, 1985

Beard JH, Malamud TJ, Rossman E: Psychiatric rehabilitation and long-term rehospitalization rates: the findings of two research studies. Schizophr Bull 4(4):622–635, 1978

Beard JH, Propst RN, Malamud TJ: The Fountain House model of rehabilitation. Psychosocial Rehabilitation Journal 5(1):47–53, 1982

Bednar RL, Lawlis GF: Empirical research in group psychotherapy, in Handbook of Psychotherapy and Behavioral Change: An Empirical Analysis. Edited by Bergin A, Garfield S. New York, John Wiley, 1971

Bellack AS, Turner SM, Hersen M, et al: An examination of the efficacy of social skills training for chronic schizophrenic patients. Hosp Community Psychiatry 35:1023–1028, 1984

Bellack AS, Morrison RL, Mueser KT: Social problem solving in schizophrenia. Schizophr Bull 15(1):101–116, 1989

Bernheim KF, Lehman AF: Working with Families of the Mentally Ill. New York, WW Norton, 1985

Bond GR: Supported work as a modification of the transitional employment model for clients with psychiatric disabilities. Psychosocial Rehabilitation Journal 11(2):55–75, 1987

Bond GR: Vocational rehabilitation for persons with severe mental illness: past, present, and future, in Rehabilitation of the Psychiatrically Disabled. Edited by Liberman RP. New York, Plenum (in press)

Bond GR, Dincin J, Setze PJ, et al: The effectiveness of psychiatric rehabilitation: a summary of research at Thresholds. Psychosocial Rehabilitation Journal 7:6–22, 1984

Bond GR, Miller LD, Krumweid RD, et al: Assertive case management in three CMHCs: a controlled study. Hosp Community Psychiatry 39(4):411–418, 1988

Borland A, McRae J, Lycan C: Outcome of five years of continuous intensive case management. Hosp Community Psychiatry 40:369–376, 1989

Brown GW, Carstairs GM, Topping G: Posthospital adjustment of chronic mental patients. Lancet 111:658–689, 1958

Brown GW, Birley JLT, Wing JK: Influence of family life on the course of schizophrenic disorders: a replication. Br J Psychiatry 121:241–258, 1972

Carmen EH, Russo NF, Miller JBK: Inequality and women's mental health: an overview. Am J Psychiatry 138:1319–1330, 1981

Carpenter WT, Schooler NR, Wise SS, et al: Treatment, services, and environmental factors. Schizophr Bull 14(3):427–437, 1988

Conners KA, Graham RS, Pulso R: Playing the store: where is the vocational in psychiatric rehabilitation? Psychosocial Rehabilitation Journal 10(3):21–33, 1987

Danley KS, Rogers ES: A psychiatric rehabilitation approach to vocational rehabilitation, in Psychiatric Rehabilitation Programs. Edited by Farkas M, Anthony WA. Baltimore, MD, Johns Hopkins University Press, 1988

Dincin J: Psychiatric rehabilitation. Schizophr Bull 1:131–148, 1975

Dincin J, Witheridge TF: Psychiatric rehabilitation as a deterrent to recidivism. Hosp Community Psychiatry 33(8):645–650, 1982

Docherty JP, van Kammen DP, Siris SG, et al: Stages of onset of schizophrenic psychosis. Am J Psychiatry 135(4):420–426, 1978

Eisenberg MG, Cole HW: A behavioral approach to job seeking for psychiatrically impaired persons. Journal of Rehabilitation Apr/May/Jun:46–49, 1986

Erikson RC: Inpatient small group psychotherapy: a survey. Clinical Psychology Review 2:137–151, 1982

Fairweather GW, Sanders D: Community Life for the Mentally Ill: An Alternative to Institutional Care. Chicago, IL, Aldine, 1969

Fairweather GW, Simon R, Gebbard MD, et al: Relative effectiveness of psychotherapeutic programs: a multicriteria comparison of four programs for three different patient groups. Psychological Monographs 74(5):1–26, 1960

Falloon IRH, Boyd JL, McGill CW, et al: Family management in the prevention of exacerbations of schizophrenia: a controlled study. N Engl J Med 306:1437–1440, 1982

Falloon IRH, Boyd JL, McGill CW, et al: Family management in the prevention of morbidity of schizophrenia. Arch Gen Psychiatry 42(9):887–896, 1985

Farkas MD, Anthony WA: Psychiatric Rehabilitation Programs: Putting Theory into Practice. Baltimore, MD, Johns Hopkins University Press, 1989

Frank AF, Gunderson JG: The role of the therapeutic alliance in the treatment of schizophrenia: relationship to course and outcome. Arch Gen Psychiatry 47(3):228–238, 1990

Fromm-Reichmann F: Notes on the development of treatment of schizophrenia by psychoanalytic psychotherapy. Psychiatry 11:263–273, 1948

Glasscote RM: Rehabilitating the Mentally Ill in the Community: A Study of Psychosocial Rehabilitation Centers. Washington, DC, Joint Information Service of the American Psychiatric Association and the National Association for Mental Health, 1971

Goering P, Wasylenki D, Lancee W, et al: From hospital to community: six-month and two-year outcomes for 505 patients. J Nerv Ment Dis 172:667–673, 1984

Goering P, Wasylenki D, Farkas M, et al: What difference does care management make? Hosp Community Psychiatry 39:272–276, 1988

Goldstein MJ, Rodnick EH, Evans JR, et al: Drug and family therapy in the aftercare of acute schizophrenics. Arch Gen Psychiatry 35(10):1169–1177, 1978

Grinspoon L, Ewalt JR, Shader RI: Schizophrenia: Pharmacotherapy and Psychotherapy. Baltimore, MD, Williams & Wilkins, 1972

Group for Advancement of Psychiatry: The Family, The Patient and The Psychiatric Hospital: Toward a New Model (Report No 117). New York, Brunner/Mazel, 1985

Gunderson JG, Frank AF, Katz HM, et al: Effects of psychotherapy in schizophrenia, II: comparative outcome of two forms of treatment. Schizophr Bull 10(4):564–598, 1984

Harding CM, Brooks GW, Ashikaga T, et al: The Vermont Longitudinal Study of persons with severe mental illness, I: methodology, study sample, and overall status 32 years later. Am J Psychiatry 144:718–726, 1987

Herz MI, Melville C: Relapse in schizophrenia. Am J Psychiatry 137(7):801–805, 1980

Hogarty GE, Anderson CM, Reiss DJ, et al: Family psychoeducation, social skills training, and maintenance chemotherapy in the aftercare treatment of schizophrenia. Arch Gen Psychiatry 43(7):633–642, 1986

Hogarty GE, McEvoy JP, Munetz M, et al: Dose of fluphenazine, familial expressed emotion, and outcome in schizophrenia. Arch Gen Psychiatry 45(9):797–805, 1988

Hoult J, Reynolds I, Charbonneau-Powis M, et al: Psychiatric hospital versus community treatment: the results of a randomized trial. Aust N Z J Psychiatry 17:160–167, 1983

Intagliata J, Willer B, Egri G: Role of the family in case management of the mentally ill. Schizophr Bull 12(4):699–708, 1986

Jacobs HE: Vocational rehabilitation, in Psychiatric Rehabilitation of Chronic Mental Patients. Edited by Liberman RP. Washington, DC, American Psychiatric Press, 1988

Kanas N: Group therapy with schizophrenics: a review of controlled studies. Int J Group Psychother 36(3):339–351, 1986

Kanas N, Stewart P, Deri J, et al: Group process in short-term outpatient therapy groups for schizophrenia. Group 13(2):67–73, 1989

Kanter J, Lamb HR, Loeper C: Expressed emotion in families: a critical review. Hosp Community Psychiatry 38(4):374–380, 1987

Karon BP, VandenBos GR: Psychotherapy of Schizophrenia: The Treatment of Choice. New York, Jason Aronson, 1981

Keith RD, Engelkes JR, Winborn BB: Employment-seeking preparation and activity: an experimental job-placement training model for rehabilitation clients. Rehabilitation Counseling Bulletin 21:159–165, 1977

Kuehnel TG, Liberman RP: Functional assessment, in Psychiatric Rehabilitation of Chronic Mental Patients. Edited by Liberman RP. Washington, DC, American Psychiatric Press, 1988

Leff J, Kuipers L, Berkowitz R, et al: A controlled trial of social interventions in the families of schizophrenic patients. Br J Psychiatry 141:121–134, 1982

Lefley HP: The family's response to mental illness in a relative, in Families of the Mentally Ill: Meeting the Challenges (New Directions for Mental Health Services, No 34). Edited by Hatfield AB. San Francisco, CA, Jossey-Bass, 1987, pp 3–21

Liberman RP: Assessment of social skills. Schizophr Bull 8:62–83, 1982a

Liberman RP: Social factors in schizophrenia, in Psychiatry 1982: The American Psychiatric Association Annual Review, Vol 1. Edited by Grinspoon L. Washington, DC, American Psychiatric Press, 1982b

Liberman RP: Psychiatric Rehabilitation of Chronic Mental Patients. Washington, DC, American Psychiatric Press, 1988

Liberman RP, Massel HK, Mosk MD, et al: Social skills training for chronic mental patients. Hosp Community Psychiatry 36(4):396–403, 1985

Liberman RP, Mueser KT, Wallace CJ, et al: Training skills in the psychiatrically disabled: learning coping and competence. Schizophr Bull 12(4):631–647, 1986

Liberman RP, DeRisi WJ, Mueser KT: Social Skills Training for Psychiatric Patients. New York, Pergamon, 1989

Lukoff D, Liberman RP, Neuchterlein KH: Symptom monitoring in the rehabilitation of schizophrenic patients. Schizophr Bull 12(4):578–603, 1986a

Lukoff D, Gioia-Hasick D, Sullivan G, et al: Sex education and rehabilitation with schizophrenic male outpatients. Schizophr Bull 12(4):669–677, 1986b

MacMillan JF, Gold A, Crow TJ, et al: Expressed emotion and relapse. Br J Psychiatry 148:133–143, 1986

Marx AJ, Test MA, Stein LI: Extrahospital management of severe mental illness. Arch Gen Psychiatry 29:505–511, 1973

May PRA: Treatment of Schizophrenia: A Comparative Study of Five Treatment Methods. New York, Science House, 1968

May PRA, Simpson GM: Schizophrenia: evaluation of treatment methods, in Comprehensive Textbook of Psychiatry, 3rd Edition, Vol 2. Edited by Kaplan HI, Freedman AM, Sadock BJ. Baltimore, MD, Williams & Wilkins, 1980, pp 1240–1275

Mechanic D: The challenge of chronic mental illness: a retrospective and prospective view. Hosp Community Psychiatry 37(9):891–896, 1986

Morrison RL, Bellack AS: Social functioning of schizophrenic patients: clinical and research issues. Schizophr Bull 13(4):715–725, 1987

Mosher LR, Keith SJ: Psychosocial treatment: Individual, group, family, and community support approaches. Schizophr Bull 6(1):10–41, 1980

Mulder R: Final Evaluation of the Harbinger Program as a Demonstration Project. Grand Rapids, MI, Kent County Community Mental Health Center, 1982

O'Brien CP: Group therapy for schizophrenia: a practical approach. Schizophr Bull 1:119–130, 1975

Olfson M: Assertive community treatment: an evaluation of the experimental evidence. Hosp Community Psychiatry 41(6):634–641, 1990

Parker G, Johnston P, Hayward L: Parental "expressed emotion" as a predictor of schizophrenic relapse. Arch Gen Psychiatry 45(9):806–813, 1988

Parloff MB, Dies RR: Group psychotherapy outcome research: 1966–1975. Int J Group Psychother 27:281–319, 1977

Rogers CR, Gendlin ET, Kiesler DJ, et al: The Therapeutic Relationship and Its Impact: Study of Psychotherapy with Schizophrenics. Madison, WI, University of Wisconsin Press, 1967

Rogers ES, Cohen BF, Danley KS, et al: Training mental health workers in psychiatric rehabilitation. Schizophr Bull 12(4):709–719, 1986

Scott D, Griffith M: The evaluation of group therapy in the treatment of schizophrenia. Small Group Behavior 13:415–422, 1982

Smyer MA, Birkel RC: Interventions with families of the chronically mentally ill elderly, in The Chronically Mentally Ill Elderly. Edited by Ligert E, Lebowitz B. Washington, DC, U.S. Government Printing Office, 1989

Spaulding WD, Storms L, Goodrich V, et al: Applications of experimental psychopathology in psychiatric rehabilitation. Schizophr Bull 12(4):560–577, 1986

Stanton AH, Gunderson JG, Knapp PH, et al: Effects of psychotherapy in schizophrenia, I: design and implementation of a controlled study. Schizophr Bull 10(4):520–563, 1984

Stein LI, Test MA: An alternative to mental hospital treatment, I: conceptual model, treatment program, and clinical evaluation. Arch Gen Psychiatry 37:393–397, 1980

Stein LI, Test MA (eds): The Training in Community Living Model: A Decade of Experience (New Directions for Mental Health Services, No 26). San Francisco, CA, Jossey-Bass, 1985

Stone WN: Treatment of the chronic mentally ill: an opportunity for the group therapist. Presidential address presented at the annual meeting of the American Group Psychotherapy Association, Boston, MA, February 20, 1990

Stotsky BA, Zolik ES: Group psychotherapy with psychotics: 1921–1963—a review. Int J Group Psychother 15:321–344, 1965

Strachan AM: Family intervention for the rehabilitation of schizophrenia: toward protection and coping. Schizophr Bull 12(4):678–698, 1986

Stratoudakis JP: Rehabilitation of the mentally ill: psychosocial, vocational, and community support perspectives. Annual Review of Rehabilitation 5:255–284, 1986

Strauss JS: Subjective experiences of schizophrenia: toward a new dynamic psychiatry—II. Schizophr Bull 15(2):179–188, 1989

Strauss JS, Loevsky L, Galzer W, et al: Organizing the complexities of schizophrenia. J Nerv Ment Dis 169:120–126, 1981

Taube CA, Morlock L, Burns BJ, et al: New directions in research on assertive community treatment. Hosp Community Psychiatry 41(6):642–647, 1990

Test MA: Continuity of care in community treatment, in Community Support Systems for the Long-Term Patient (New Directions for Mental Health Services, No 2). Edited by Stein LI. San Francisco, CA, Jossey-Bass, 1979, pp 15–23

Test MA, Knoedler WH, Allness DJ, et al: Characteristics of young adults with schizophrenic disorders treated in the community. Hosp Community Psychiatry 36(8):853–858, 1985

Vaughn CE, Leff JP: The influence of family and social factors on the course of psychiatric illness. Br J Psychiatry 129:125–137, 1976

Vaughn CE, Snyder KS, Jones S, et al: Family factors in schizophrenic relapse: replication in California of British research on expressed emotion. Arch Gen Psychiatry 41:1169–1177, 1984

Wallace CJ: Functional assessment in rehabilitation. Schizophr Bull 12(4):604–630, 1986

Wallace CJ, Liberman RP: Social skills training for patients with schizophrenia: a controlled clinical trial. Psychiatry Res 15:239–247, 1985

Wasylenki D, Goering P, Lancee W, et al: Psychiatric aftercare in a metropolitan setting. Can J Psychiatry 30:329–336, 1985

Wehman P, Moon MS: Vocational Rehabilitation and Supported Employment. Baltimore, MD, Brookes, 1988

Witheridge TF: The role of the Thresholds Bridge Outreach worker: implications for professional social work training. Paper presented at Wingspread, Racine, WI, May 23–24, 1985

Wright RG, Heiman JR, Shupe J, et al: Defining and measuring stabilization of patients during four years of intensive community support. Am J Psychiatry 146:1293–1298, 1989

Yalom ID: Inpatient Group Psychotherapy. New York, Basic Books, 1983

Zeldow PB: Sex differences in psychiatric evaluation and treatment. Arch Gen Psychiatry 35:89–93, 1978

6

Implications for Organizing and Financing Care for People With Chronic Mental Illness

Dramatic changes in public mental health programs since World War II reflect changes in the delivery of all health care. These have been described by Starr (1982) as "the transformation of American medicine." Along with new therapies to treat major psychiatric disorders have come diversification, specialization and expansion of the mental health professions, introduction of private and public health insurance plans, the growth of the hospital industry, and a shift toward ambulatory care. Furthermore, the removal of patients from long-term care asylums over the last 40 years has separated the treatment of patients from the provision of basic social welfare services. Since deinstitutionalization, these services somehow were expected to be provided by community agencies. These changes in general health and human services policy have had a profound impact on the organization and financing of public mental health services, and they raise major issues for mental health policy.

Despite a growth in the size of state mental health departments and in the number of institutions, programs, and providers directed toward psychiatric care, many people, especially those who are seriously mentally ill, still do not receive the care they need. The tasks of coordinating the disparate community-based services and integrating the individualized needs of patients with schizophrenia and other chronic mental illnesses have been largely unsuccessful. A pressing need exists to find

---

Portions of this chapter are adapted from contributions by two GAP Committee members (Robert Dorwart and Howard Goldman) to the NIMH National Plan of Research to Improve Services (1991).

more effective ways to integrate fragmented services within the existing service systems.

In this chapter, which is organized into two major sections, we discuss the separate but related problems of the organization and financing of mental health care. The first section addresses the problem of the fragmentation of care and proposes five mechanisms for integrating services. The second describes several major programs for financing services and makes recommendations concerning each.

Organizing Care

Fragmentation as a Systems Problem

Despite widespread agreement on the basic elements of services needed by people with serious mental illnesses, including those with schizophrenia, one of the most striking organizational features of mental health care systems in the United States is the diversity across and within state and local programs (Mechanic 1987; Torrey et al. 1990). Although this diversity is attributable to the many historical, political, social, scientific, and economic forces that have influenced the evolution of our mental health care systems, it also reflects society's attempts to meet the multiple needs of individuals with major and often lifelong illnesses or disability.

Grob (1979) described the long-running debate over whether a medical or a psychosocial model is preferable in responding to the needs of the mentally ill. The debate continues to some extent today. Where should individuals with severe mental illness be treated: in specialty hospitals, general hospitals, community residential programs, ambulatory care centers, or family settings? In addition, available services are often mismatched to the needs of the individuals who use them (Mechanic 1987; Torrey 1988; Torrey et al. 1990).

The service provision problems of today's mental health care system, however, go far beyond a conflict between medical and psychosocial treatment approaches. Indeed, there is a lack of scientific data and of agreement about what services are needed for whom, how best to organize these services, and who should provide and pay for them. Fragmentation is a phenomenon that presents a threat to access and continuity of care, to efficiency and cost-effectiveness of services, and to planning, policy making, and management of programs.

Because so many mental health services depend on large public programs, we need to better understand the governmental structures (federal government agencies, state mental health authorities, and county, municipal, and local jurisdictions) and policy-making processes that determine how care is provided. Political science, public finance, and management studies can help us analyze the structure of state mental health authorities so that we may devise strategies for effective change in planning and program implementation.

In addition to medical needs that sometimes include hospital stays for acute crises or safety, patients often require a wide array of socioeconomic supports, such as housing, subsistence, social service, counseling, and transportation. These basic dependency needs, related to the patients' disabilities, are by no means unique to those who suffer from psychiatric disorders. In fact, they are associated with people who have widely different diseases and statuses: those who have chronic medical illnesses, major physical handicaps, disabilities of advanced old age, or very young children in inadequate families or who are victims of economic dislocation. Thus, people with major mental illnesses may, like others with long-term disability, require services. These include income support, vocational rehabilitation, assistance in activities of daily living, structured or supervised accommodations, psychoeducational supports for family, help in choosing self-care treatment options, and access to an appropriate array of medical, psychiatric, and preventive care services.

Integration of Care

Meeting the complex multiple needs of people with schizophrenia requires an integrated system of care. Solving the problem of matching services to the long-term, changing needs of individuals calls for creativity, innovation, collaboration, and expanded efforts to research and evaluate the effectiveness of organized mental health service systems and individual treatment practices (Taube et al. 1989).

Patient care in the public mental health system in the United States involves significant federal government responsibility; a massive state or county role; a decentralized, often uncoordinated local mental health center role; and a poorly integrated role for private providers and office-based practitioners. The most familiar problems are seen in the tension between state hospitals and local community mental health centers over their respective roles in coordinating care. In some locales, a comprehensive array of inpatient and outpatient services is coordinated for an entire catchment area. In other places, the catchment area concept artificially and ineffectively sets the boundary for a loosely configured collection of state and local hospitals, community programs, and private providers, with little or no central authority or integration of care (Group for the Advancement of Psychiatry 1983).

To address this problem in large urban areas, the Robert Wood Johnson (RWJ) Foundation has initiated a national, nine-city demonstration project to show how a new centralized administrative authority can improve the financing and organizing of care for the chronically mentally ill (Goldman et al. 1990a, 1990b; Shore and Cohen 1990). The new entities may be private, nonprofit corporations or quasi-public authorities. The evaluation of the RWJ demonstration projects is being carried out in collaboration with the National Institute of Mental Health (NIMH) in an excellent example of multidisciplinary, multisite service systems research.

A significant aspect of the program involves housing subsidies provided by the federal government. The goal of the program is to demonstrate that by incorporating elements of successful mental health programs and a comprehensive range of services, patients can live independently relying on services provided by "a single mental health authority." The demonstration posits that such a mental health organization must include the following five critical elements:

1. There is a single point of clinical, administrative, and fiscal responsibility.
2. For each patient, there is a designated caregiver who is responsible for coordinating the various components of the service system.
3. Flexible financing is available.
4. The development of a range of housing options for people with chronic mental illness is desirable.
5. A range of psychosocial and vocational rehabilitation programs are needed to support patients in the community.

The cornerstone of these demonstration projects is the creation of a central agency or single mental health authority to coordinate and integrate the services provided to individual patients. In each city, the single authority takes a different concrete organizational form, but in each it involves consolidation and centralization of authority into a single (often new) entity.

There have been many attempts to introduce integration and coordination into the service system. For example, the NIMH-sponsored Community Support Program was developed in the 1980s in order to provide continuity of social services for people with chronic mental illness in community settings (Tessler and Goldman 1982). Among the most widely employed strategies are the following approaches:

- Greater involvement of family members in treatment planning;

- Introduction of case managers (variously defined) into the service system to coordinate care, especially for seriously mentally ill people living in the community;
- Development of training in community living skills for patients;
- Linkage of mental health programs to other services appropriate to client needs, such as social service and housing agencies, the criminal justice system, chemical dependency treatment facilities, vocational training, and so forth; and
- Fiscal incentives toward integration of care, such as capitation plans.

The following subsections provide more information on and suggest directions for further research for each of these approaches.

Family support systems. Better ways are needed to involve family members of people who are mentally ill with service systems, in treatment planning, and with policy-making and advocacy processes (Group for the Advancement of Psychiatry 1989). The recently formed National Alliance for the Mentally Ill has made progress in integrating families into the treatment process (Shetler 1986). The NIMH is creating a national center for research on self-help resources; sustaining the center will depend to a large extent on help from family members. More research is needed to assess the most effective roles and responsibilities for family members in the planning, governance, support, and monitoring of services. The role of families in providing social and financial support for patients must be recognized by mental health care providers, who should focus research on ways in which they can work with, support, and better understand the families' problems in coping with mentally ill relatives.

Case management. Case management is not new to mental health services. Community mental health centers and community support programs have for years recognized the need for trained personnel who could help people who are mentally ill find suitable aid and who could then follow up on treatment (Tessler and Goldman 1982). Recently there has been increased interest and insistence on case management for people with severe mental illness (Robinson and Bergman 1989). The Omnibus Budget Reconciliation Act of 1986 encourages the use of case management for chronically mentally ill or disabled people who receive Medicaid, recognizing its usefulness in coordinating services. Case managers operate in a manner similar to social caseworkers: increasing an individual patient's access to appropriate services, facilitating and monitoring specialized care, and providing a responsible and consistent interpersonal contact between the individual and the service system. So far, there have been few carefully designed studies of the effectiveness and the costs versus benefits of different models of case management, even though their widespread use by state and local mental health authorities affords ample opportunity to test hypotheses about their impact.

Rehabilitation approaches. As noted by Anthony and Branch (1989), for over a decade there has been a developing base of research examining community support programs and rehabilitation services. Using largely quasi-experimental designs, such components of community support systems have been studied as outreach, treatment, health care, housing, peer support, crisis intervention, and rehabilitation services. Some of these topics overlap with broad social policy studies into such social welfare issues as housing and unemployment. Other studies are focused on specific models for reducing the long-term disability by increasing the socialization skills of people with severe mental disorders. Early reports from the study of the federally funded Community Support Program are encouraging; according to Mulkern and Manderscheid (1989), the number of patients served grew from about 4,000 in 1980 to 350,000 in 1984 while meeting the program's mandate to serve those who were most severely disabled.

System linkages. In the absence of strong federal leadership, the major locus of policies concerning the long-term care of individuals with severe mental disorders has shifted to state and local governments. Numerous approaches have been tried and evaluated to increase service system linkages. Some have been broadly based on reforms in legislation such as those in Ohio (Goldman et al. 1990b; Morrissey et al. 1990). At least two approaches rely on introducing new forms of financing services, as in Dane County, Wisconsin, or Rochester, New York (Marshall 1988). Others involve a realignment of authority using public authorities or restructured local mental health centers. Still others rely on case managers and administrative arrangements, such as contracting for services to expand interorganizational arrangements, sharing of services, and so forth. Creating innovative services to meet multiple needs, such as a "dual-diagnosis unit" of a hospital or a specialty clinic, is yet another approach to linking otherwise separate programs.

Fiscal incentives. State and community programs provide the crucible for problem solving and innovation as well as the context for the provision of programs of treatment and care. As an example, in 1988, Governor Richard F. Celeste of Ohio signed into law a new mental health act. This legislation reflected political and professional consensus about needed reforms in the mental health care system. Under the statute, state care of severely mentally ill people was reorganized and redesigned with respect to control, funding, and location of service. The law sought 1) to integrate control of hospital and community care under local community (county) citizen boards; 2) to redefine the role of the state agency as the funder and monitor of services; 3) to create financial incentives for the development of alternatives to hospitalization; 4) to reduce reliance on state hospitals in favor of competitive arrangements with local community general hospitals; and 5) to revise laws governing care of the mentally ill to make services more humane and less restrictive.

A centerpiece of the Ohio plan is a provision for purchase-of-service contracting with community agencies for a range of state-supported services. Under this plan, services are paid for but not necessarily provided by the state. A public-private partnership is possible, and the funds "follow the patients" as they move from institutional to community-based care and, when necessary, back again. The Ohio example illustrates across-the-board reform of state mental health policies and includes not only program change but also long-term systemic investment in mental health services, including training, research, regulation, and local, decentralized community development.

According to the preliminary report of a legislative study group of outside experts who have studied the implementation of the Ohio Mental Health Act of 1988, significant progress has been made by the system since the passage of the act (Ohio Legislature Preliminary Report 1991). The state hospital population has been reduced by approximately 30%. Residential, crisis, and case management services have been dramatically increased, with significant funds being shifted from institutional to community-based services. In the first 18 months of the implementation, the decrease in hospital days was primarily due to a reduced length of stay for long-term patients, not for short-stay patients, which indicates some change in clinical practices. One of Ohio's 15 state mental hospitals has been closed. A newly elected governor and a new state commissioner of mental health are proceeding with further implementation of the act based on early demonstrated feasibility to reform the systems of care.

Just as we have identified a need for better integration of services to improve the care for severely mentally ill people, so, too, would we stress the need for integration in the financing of service systems. In the following section, we discuss the major ways in which mental health services are currently funded and recommend changes that would foster better continuity and system coordination.

Financing Care

Today's new and more optimistic view of the long-term outcome of severe mental illnesses such as schizophrenia requires a reconceptualization of systems of care and, as a result, a new plan for financing that care. We suggest that current expenditures would be more efficiently invested in shorter, more focused acute interventions, coupled with more generous support to meet basic needs and to provide aggressive habilitation and rehabilitation. A system of financing long-term care should provide the resources to meet five service objectives:

1. Basic support (food, clothing, shelter, or stable income) to promote survival, reduce secondary morbidity, and improve quality of life;
2. Treatment of complications, such as alcohol or other drug abuse, and intercurrent illnesses to reduce morbidity and mortality;
3. Acute treatment of life-threatening episodes to prevent suicide and minimize the aftereffects of acute psychotic disorganization;
4. Rehabilitation to compensate for lost function and productivity, or habilitation to teach basic skills; and
5. A system of long-term continuous therapeutic interventions to guide patients and their families through the lifelong course of the illness and the various stages of recovery.

Recommendations to Improve Financing Mechanisms

In spite of a climate of fiscal conservatism, there are a number of existing mechanisms that could be used to finance the long-term care of patients with schizophrenia and other disabling mental illnesses. We recommend expanding access to the resources offered by a variety of federal agencies (Health Care Financing Administration, Housing and Urban Development, Social Security Administration, and Department of Veterans Affairs); and we suggest several changes in these financing mechanisms. Further research is needed to assess innovative models for financing appropriate, cost-effective mental health care. We recommend adopting the research agenda in this area proposed by the NIMH's (1991) National Plan of Research to Improve Services.

U.S. Department of Housing and Urban Development. There are several housing rent subsidy programs operated by the U.S. Department of Housing and Urban Development (HUD) that could be used to help chronically mentally ill people afford and obtain better housing (Goldman and Newman 1990; National Institute of Mental Health 1990). However, HUD and local public housing authorities would have to be willing to work with mental health authorities to develop support systems for mentally ill patients living in subsidized housing—an effort that has seldom been made in the past. Support must be provided to landlords, as well as residents, if these programs are to be successful. HUD subsidies vary: sometimes the certificates or vouchers are issued to the patient and sometimes to the housing unit. A project-based certificate could be held by a mental health authority and used to provide a subsidized rental unit for a patient participating in a treatment or rehabilitation program. Until the RWJ Foundation-HUD Program on Chronic Mental Illness made 125 HUD certificates available to each of the nine demonstration cities, public housing authorities had received little encouragement from HUD to provide special assistance to the mentally ill (Aiken et al. 1987; Goldman and Newman 1990; National Institute of Mental Health 1990).

Much can be learned from the Program on Chronic Mental Illness and similar demonstration programs about the best ways to implement and support housing for mentally ill people. On the other hand, it does not require a demonstration project to know that a man or woman with schizophrenia or other severe mental illness is better off inside than outside in the winter. HUD could be persuaded to marshal its resources to provide rent subsidies to indigent mentally ill individuals so that they can afford proper shelter. In turn, the mental health community would have to make a commitment to use more of its resources to support its clients in community-based housing.

Social Security Administration. Many individuals who are mentally disabled and eligible for Social Security Disability Insurance (SSDI) benefits or Supplemental Security Income (SSI) are not enrolled in these programs (Goldman and Manderscheid 1987; Lave and Goldman 1990; Taube et al. 1990). Patients with serious mental illness have difficulty negotiating the complex application process and, until recently, faced outmoded standards for assessing their impairments and ability to work. Recent changes in the standards for evaluating claims of mental impairment have eased the process somewhat. The Social Security Administration (SSA) has also revised its process to reduce the time needed to adjudicate claims, but these changes have not been well implemented.

Given the magnitude of the problem of providing needed income support for disabled mentally ill individuals, SSA could operate its existing mechanisms better to facilitate access to benefits, reduce processing time, and improve the accuracy and efficiency of the process, and it could add aggressive outreach to its list of responsibilities. In addition, SSA could make widely known and available the use of representative payees, work incentive programs, trial work periods, and other programs to facilitate rehabilitation activities. Many of these innovations are available from SSA, but mental health providers lack the knowledge or understanding of them. Mental health personnel must become better informed about Social Security benefits, and we can only hope that SSA will respond to this need for better information.

Department of Veterans Affairs. The Department of Veterans Affairs (VA) has developed a number of demonstration programs for people who are chronically mentally ill and/or homeless (Rosenheck and Fischer 1990). They focus on supplying basic needs as well as on mental health treatment. Perhaps the most fundamental problem with the approach of the VA to the care of mentally ill people has been its discrimination against paying benefits to individuals disabled by alcohol or other drug abuse (Ridgely et al. 1990). This may limit the access of chronically mentally ill people who are also substance abusers to the income support that they need.

Medicare. Medicare is fundamentally problematic for the care of chronically mentally ill people because of the explicit focus of the program on acute medical care rather than on rehabilitation or maintenance therapy. Medicare pays for treatment of the acute exacerbations of chronic mental illness, but it pays very little for ongoing care (Goldman and Manderscheid 1987; Goldman et al. 1987). Limits on care for chronic patients have meant that it can be difficult (or impossible) to get Medicare to reimburse partial hospitalization programs, nursing home stays, and extended stays in psychiatric hospitals.

A few recent changes have helped patients who are chronically mentally ill gain needed coverage under Medicare. In particular, benefits for the "medical management" of patients on psychotropic medications now match those for all general medical services, which indicates recognition that those with mental problems deserve more equal treatment than they have received in the past. The recent expansion of dollar limits on ambulatory coverage of mental illness care is another step in the right direction. Efforts must be made to remove the 190-day lifetime limitation on care in freestanding hospitals without imposing annual limits, which are likely to affect those chronically mentally ill patients who are often hospitalized (Lave and Goldman 1990).

A more far-reaching policy recommendation would be to expand Medicare to provide long-term care for everyone eligible. The fate of the catastrophic coverage provisions under Medicare, passed and then repealed by the 101st Congress, suggests that such additional coverage, if it required higher payments by beneficiaries, is not likely to be legislated. However, efforts should be mounted to ensure that any plans developed for long-term care (perhaps under commercial insurance) include mentally ill people along with other segments of the population (Pepper Commission 1990).

Medicaid. Medicaid has a broad benefit structure but pays too little, in most states, to encourage providers to participate. This is especially true of outpatient services. In addition, many poor and disabled individuals are not enrolled in Medicaid, both because eligibility standards have been tightened and because mentally ill individuals have had difficulty with the enrollment process (Taube et al. 1990). Reimbursable services are usually tied to office-based practice and do not permit reimbursement for services provided to patients outside of formal service settings. Research on the effectiveness of assertive community treatment (Stein and Test 1985) provides evidence that community-based service is extremely beneficial in reducing the severity of symptoms and disability associated with chronic illness.

We recommend that special efforts be made to assist mentally ill people who might be eligible to apply for SSI and Medicaid, including creating financial incentives for individual providers to assist their patients with the application process. Adequate fees should be paid to encourage providers to meet the broad array of needs of the chronic patient, including gaining access to social welfare and medical services. This may mean providing case management services by trained social service aides as a mandatory benefit, permitting off-site care, and reimbursing comprehensive services within a case management model. It is also critical that the Medicaid program provide for the treatment of substance abuse. Accomplishing these goals will require policy changes at the state level, unless additional mandates are included in future federal legislation.

The Federal Block Grant. The federal block grant to the states for mental health, drug, and alcohol abuse treatment could be used in a targeted fashion to support the care of chronically mentally ill people with alcohol and other substance abuse problems. Resources could be set aside for demonstration projects on the care of people with dual diagnoses—projects similar to those of Lehman and colleagues (1989) and Drake and colleagues (1990). The federal government could work to coordinate the use of the block grant among the three federal institutes within the Alcohol, Drug Abuse and Mental Health Administration. It should also insist that the same be done among agencies at the state level, in order to facilitate joint management of the problems of mentally ill patients with substance abuse problems (Ridgely et al. 1990).

Recommendations for Research on Organizing and Financing Care

NIMH (1991) recently convened panels of experts to develop recommendations for research on the care of severely mentally ill people. One set of recommendations concerns clinical services research. Epidemiological studies, such as the long-term, natural history investigation of the severe mental disorders, are needed to determine predictors of clinical course and potential response to early intervention and treatment. Indeed, the report notes that epidemiological studies focusing on disability itself are needed. Another specific recommendation is for a housing census of living arrangements used by people with severe mental disorders. In addition, the panel recommends not only further research on somatic therapies, psychotherapies, and sociotherapies but also research on combining or linking treatment and rehabilitation modalities and on explicating the different long-term outcomes of each. Specifically, the panel recommends further work in developing and evaluating methods and measures for the study of the many dimensions of continuity and integration of care involving rehabilitation, vocational activities, and residential services.

In addition to clinical services research, there is a need for service systems research. This research should, according to the NIMH (1991) report, focus on several general topics: identification of service needs, legal issues, human resource development, overcoming stigma, and the organization and financing of mental health care at the local and national levels. This research should be directed toward answering broad questions, such as how services should be organized and provided to ensure the best outcomes. In recognition of the diversity of state-based programs and policies concerning treatment for patients with disorders such as schizophrenia, studies need to focus on existing community models and the study of new ones. There is also a need for a range of innovative models that will fit with the requirements of state Medicaid programs and differently organized state mental health authorities. Ultimately, the goal of such a proposed research program would be to make possible a national community-based system of care for severely mentally ill people that can intervene early and effectively to reduce the level of disability associated with severe mental illness (National Institute of Mental Health 1991).

Conclusions

Overall, the mental health service system in this country needs to be modified to become less fragmented and more responsive to the needs of individuals with severe mental illness. The system of financing can be changed in many ways. Beyond shifting resources within the mental health care system, existing resources for income support and housing are available and could be better utilized to meet the basic survival needs of those with disabling mental illnesses. These changes can significantly improve the long-term outcomes for this population.

References

Aiken L, Somers S, Shore M: Private foundations in health affairs: a case study of the development of a national initiative for the chronically mentally ill. Am Psychol 41:1290–1295, 1987

Anthony WA, Branch A: Research on community support systems: what have we learned? Psychosocial Rehabilitation Journal 12:55–81, 1989

Drake RE, Osher FC, Noordsy DL, et al: Diagnosis of alcohol use disorders in schizophrenia. Schizophr Bull 16(1):57–67, 1990

Goldman HH, Manderscheid RW: Chronic mental disorder in the United States, in Mental Health U.S.—1987 (DHHS Publ No ADM-87-1518). Edited by Manderscheid RW, Barrett SA. Washington, DC, U.S. Government Printing Office, 1987

Goldman HH, Newman S: Financing and reimbursement issues, in Homelessness and Mental Illness: Toward the Next Generation of Research Studies. Edited by Morrissey J, Dennis D. Rockville, MD, National Institute of Mental Health, 1990

Goldman HH, Taube CA, Jencks SF: The organization of the psychiatric inpatient services system. Medical Care Supplement 25(9):S6–S21, 1987

Goldman HH, Lehman AF, Morrissey JP, et al: Design for the national evaluation of the Robert Wood Johnson Foundation program on chronic mental illness. Hosp Community Psychiatry 41:1217–1221, 1990a

Goldman HH, Morrissey JP, Ridgely MS: Form and function of mental health authorities at RWJ Foundation sites: preliminary observations. Hosp Community Psychiatry 41:1222–1229, 1990b

Grob G: Rediscovering asylums: the unhistorical history of the mental hospital, in The Therapeutic Revolution: Essays in the Social History of American Medicine. Edited by Vogel B, Rosenberg I. Philadelphia, PA, University of Pennsylvania Press, 1979

Group for the Advancement of Psychiatry: Community Psychiatry: A Reappraisal (Report No 113). New York, Mental Health Materials Center, 1983

Group for the Advancement of Psychiatry: Psychiatric Prevention and the Family Life Cycle (Report No 127). New York, Brunner/Mazel, 1989

Lave JR, Goldman HH: Medicare and the financing of mental disorders. Health Affairs 9(1):5–18, 1990

Lehman AF, Myers CP, Corty E: Assessment and classification of patients with psychiatric and substance abuse syndromes. Hosp Community Psychiatry 40(10):1019–1024, 1989

Marshall P: A Community Care System for the Mentally Ill. Rochester, NY, Integrated Mental Health, 1988

Mechanic D: Correcting misperceptions in mental health policy: strategies for improved care of the seriously mentally ill. Milbank Q 65(2):203–230, 1987

Morrissey JP, Tausig M, Lindsey ML: Network Analysis Methods for Mental Health Service System Research: A Comparison of Two Community Support Systems. National Institute of Mental Health Series BN, No 6 (DHHS Publ No ADM-85-1383). Washington, DC, U.S. Government Printing Office, 1990

Mulkern VM, Manderscheid RW: Characteristics of community support program clients in 1980 and 1984. Hospital Community Psychiatry 40(2):165–172, 1989

National Institute of Mental Health: Request for applications, MH-90-14, McKinney Research Demonstration Program for Homeless Mentally Ill. Rockville, MD, National Institute of Mental Health, 1990

National Institute of Mental Health: Caring for people with severe mental disorders: A national plan of research to improve services (DHHS Publ No ADM-91-1762). Washington, DC, U.S. Government Printing Office, 1991

Ohio Legislature: Legislative Summary: Implementation of the Ohio Mental Health Act of 1988. Columbus, OH, Preliminary Report of the Study Committee on Mental Health Services, 1991

Pepper Commission: A Call for Action. Washington, DC, U.S. Government Printing Office, 1990

Ridgely MS, Goldman HH, Willenbring M: Barriers to the cost of persons with dual diagnoses: organizational and financing issues. Schizophr Bull 16(1):123–132, 1990

Robinson G, Bergman GT: Choices in Case Management: A Review of Current Knowledge and Practice in Mental Health Programs. Washington, DC, Policy Resources, 1989

Rosenheck R, Fischer P: Longitudinal designs, in Homelessness and Mental Illness: Toward the Next Generation of Research Studies. Edited by Morrissey J, Dennis D. Rockville, MD, National Institute of Mental Health, 1990

Shetler H: A History of the National Alliance for the Mentally Ill. Arlington, VA, National Alliance for the Mentally Ill, 1986

Shore FM, Cohen MD: The Robert Wood Johnson Foundation program on chronic mental illness: an overview. Hosp Community Psychiatry 41:1212–1216, 1990

Starr P: The Social Transformation of American Medicine. New York, Basic Books, 1982

Stein LI, Test MA (eds): The Training in Community Living Model: Decade of Experience (New Directions for Mental Health Services No 26). San Francisco, CA, Jossey-Bass, 1985

Taube CA, Mechanic D, Hohmann A (eds): The Future of Mental Health Services Research. National Institute of Mental Health (DHHS Publ No ADM-89-1600). Washington, DC, U.S. Government Printing Office, 1989

Taube CA, Goldman HH, Salkever D: Medicaid coverage for mental illness: balancing access and costs. Health Affairs 9(1):19–30, 1990

Tessler RC, Goldman HH: The Chronically Mentally Ill: Assessing Community Support Programs. Cambridge, MA, Ballinger, 1982

Torrey EF: Nowhere to Go: The Tragic Odyssey of the Homeless Mentally Ill. New York, Harper & Row, 1988

Torrey EF, Wolfe SM, Flynn L: Care of the Seriously Mentally Ill: A Rating of State Programs, 3rd Edition. Washington, DC, Public Citizen Health Research Group and the National Alliance for the Mentally Ill, 1990

7

Recommendations: Looking Toward the Future

In this book, we indicate the need for a new focus for the contemporary treatment of individuals with schizophrenia. A longitudinal perspective reveals that current approaches have overemphasized the suppression of acute, disruptive symptoms and have underappreciated the potential for long-term adjustment of individuals with schizophrenia. Acute treatment should be combined with an ongoing program of care and support for these patients, and this program should include medication maintenance, psychosocial and family interventions, treatment for alcohol and other drug abuse, social welfare support, and active rehabilitation.

In reframing our notions about how to help people with schizophrenia, we must consider the natural course of the illness, phases of adult development, and emerging strategies of pharmacotherapeutic and psychosocial interventions. When we look at all these elements, it is evident that the existing care system fails to meet the changing needs of this patient population. It is also clear that the continuing development and dissemination of treatment for people with schizophrenia will occur under the influence of three prevailing forces in the 1990s: the rapidly evolving brain sciences, the growing advocacy of psychosocial services for people with severe mental illnesses, and the pressing economic concern that health and human service dollars be spent judiciously.

An adult developmental perspective shifts the focus from short-term, crisis-oriented, symptom-focused management of patients with schizophrenia to a longitudinal approach. In this chapter, we summarize the implications that this longitudinal perspective brings to the challenge of providing better treatment to these patients.

The Adult Developmental Perspective: Future Directions

In looking beyond symptom suppression, the following areas require further study:

1. The developmental perspective underscores the need for a better understanding not only of the early, acute, active phase of schizophrenic illness but also of the quiescent later years that constitute most of the schizophrenic individual's adult life.
2. We must learn more about the efficacy and synergy of different therapeutic and rehabilitative modalities during the various phases of the illness in order to guide the timing and integration of different services and treatment interventions.
3. Further consideration must be given to goal setting and active intervention later in the illness when greater stability may increase the patient's opportunities for growth and enhanced quality of life.
4. Significant differences between the life experiences of men and women with schizophrenia must be taken into account in planning treatment and rehabilitation.

The Postinstitutional Generation

People with schizophrenia are extremely vulnerable to some of the hazards of modern life. They often lack the ability to obtain critical life resources and supports independently.

In the era of institutionalization, housing, food, health care, and protection from many of the hazards of daily "community" life were provided. But these social welfare services were uncoupled from treatment services and generally neglected in the transition from institution-based care to community-based care. Nevertheless, such services are essential for successful treatment and must be provided as a necessary first step.

In addition, contemporary community life poses special life- and treatment-threatening hazards for people with schizophrenia. Their increasing exposure to alcohol, other drugs, AIDS, violent crime, and victimization of all sorts must be prevented. Substance abuse and dependence must be treated as a core component of mental health services.

Pharmacotherapeutic Interventions

The most effective use of medication beyond the acute phase of schizophrenia requires that clinicians weigh the benefits of symptom control against the potential adverse psychosocial and somatic effects of the medications. The ultimate value of pharmacotherapy can be increased by the longitudinal perspective, which emphasizes consideration of issues such as the following:

1. In contrast to the ways in which neuroleptic medication is used to suppress acute disruptive schizophrenic symptoms, a less aggressive approach is feasible during periods of remission. Further investigation of low-dosage and targeted-dosing strategies is worth pursuing. Compared with traditional dosing approaches, these alternate strategies may offer significant long-term social and vocational benefits.
2. Tardive dyskinesia, akathisia, and akinesia, among other adverse medication effects, can interfere with long-term social and vocational functioning. Through research and education, clinicians can enhance awareness of these effects and seek more effective ways to limit or counteract them.
3. Depression, akinesia, and agoraphobia accompanying panic disorder can mimic the so-called negative or deficit symptoms of schizophrenia. Clinicians need to give thoughtful attention to the differential diagnosis of people with schizophrenia who appear withdrawn or unmotivated.
4. Adjunctive and new medications may have important long-term benefits by suppressing residual positive symptoms, alleviating persistent negative symptoms, treating patients unresponsive to current approaches, and targeting treatable secondary syndromes such as depression or panic disorder.
5. Clinicians must advocate the development of new medications and the facilitation of patients' access to new modes of treatment.
6. Through practice and teaching, clinicians can support the integration of pharmacologic and psychosocial interventions to maximize outcomes through various phases of schizophrenia.

Psychosocial Interventions

Most people with schizophrenia suffer serious social and occupational dysfunction. The following issues in the area of psychosocial interventions should be considered:

1. Opportunities for longitudinal relationships between patient and treatment providers (psychiatrists, therapists, and case managers) should be facilitated and maintained.

2. Group experiences (whether in the context of group therapy, rehabilitation services in a group setting, or self-help groups) should be used more frequently to enhance patients' self-esteem and improve social role functioning.
3. Professionals need to understand and acknowledge the significant influence of families and the burden they bear in the care of these patients. We must provide families with necessary and sufficient resources, including helping them to develop the skills required to cope effectively with their ill relatives.
4. The critical components and characteristics of effective psychosocial interventions should be identified. These interventions should be modified to accommodate variability in patients' age, gender, race, developmental level, intelligence, culture, family situation, and locale.
5. More personnel should be trained and more appropriate educational programs developed in order to meet the psychosocial needs of these patients (Group for the Advancement of Psychiatry, in press).
6. Programs to establish work, social, and living environments appropriate to the needs and competencies of individuals with schizophrenia should be further developed and orchestrated in a manner appropriate to their capacities and life phases.
7. Individuals with schizophrenia should be included as active collaborators in establishing goals that guide the content, combination, and timing of their treatment, rehabilitation, and support services.
8. We must remain attentive to and help patients overcome both the internal and external barriers keeping them from recovery.

Organizing and Financing Care

The long-term outcome for individuals with schizophrenia is undermined by inadequate long-term support, particularly in relation to such complications of chronic illness as homelessness, medical illness, and substance abuse. Although many of the recommendations reviewed in this book would be endorsed by competent clinicians, too often those same recommendations are not carried out. Our recommendations for the organizing and financing of care and treatment of individuals with schizophrenia include the following:

1. A system of care should include social welfare as well as treatment services.

2. Treatment services should be expanded to include habilitation and rehabilitation services.
3. Patients, their family members, and their advocacy organizations should be involved in planning the system of care.
4. Responsibility for the care of individuals with chronic mental illness should be centralized in order to integrate mental health, alcohol, and other drug abuse treatments with general health, social welfare, and housing services and their agencies. At the organizational level, this integration may take the form of a centralized authority. At the clinical services level, it may take the form of clinically sensitive case management.
5. Access to entitlements, income support, and linked health care benefits should be increased.
6. Current housing subsidies for people with disabling mental illness should be accessed, and the total number of housing units should be increased.
7. Barriers to appropriate services should be removed from existing health care financing.
8. Knowledge from new research based on innovative service demonstration programs should be made available to mental health administrators and policymakers.
9. Finally, we need to supplement our scarce health care resources with an adequate supply of other human services resources for income support, vocational rehabilitation, housing, and other aspects of social welfare.

Conclusions

We have reason to be guardedly optimistic with regard to the long-term outcomes of people with schizophrenia. We stand the best chance of realizing this optimism

- By adopting a longitudinal perspective;
- By attending to the multiple domains of adjustment; and
- By advocating the funding and accessibility of the appropriate and necessary social services.

References

Group for the Advancement of Psychiatry: A Resident's Guide to the Treatment of Patients With Chronic Mental Illness. (in press)

GAP Committees and Membership

Committee on Adolescence

Warren J. Gadpaille, Denver, CO, *Chairperson*
Hector R. Bird, New York, NY
Ian A. Canino, New York, NY
Michael G. Kalogerakis, New York, NY
Paulina F. Kernberg, New York, NY
Clarice J. Kestenbaum, New York, NY
Richard C. Marohn, Chicago, IL
Silvio J. Onesti, Jr., Belmont, MA

Committee on Aging

Gene D. Cohen, Washington, DC, *Chairperson*
Karen Blank, West Hartford, CT
Eric D. Caine, Rochester, NY
Charles M. Gaitz, Houston, TX
Gary Gottlieb, Los Angeles, CA
Ira R. Katz, Philadelphia, PA
Andrew F. Leuchter, Los Angeles, CA
Gabe J. Maletta, Minneapolis, MN
Richard A. Margolin, Nashville, TN
George H. Pollock, Chicago, IL
Kenneth M. Sakauye, New Orleans, LA
Charles A. Shamoian, Larchmont, NY
F. Conyers Thompson, Jr., Atlanta, GA

Committee on Alcoholism and the Addictions

Joseph Westermeyer, Minneapolis, MN, *Chairperson*
Margaret H. Bean-Bayog, Lexington, MA
Susan J. Blumenthal, Washington, DC
Richard J. Frances, Newark, NJ
Marc Galanter, New York, NY
Edward J. Khantzian, Haverhill, MA
Earl A. Loomis, Jr., Augusta, GA
Sheldon I. Miller, Chicago, IL
Steven M. Mirin, Belmont, MA

Edgar P. Nace, Dallas, TX
Norman L. Paul, Lexington, MA
Peter Steinglass, Washington, DC
John S. Tamerin, Greenwich, CT

Committee on Child Psychiatry

Peter E. Tanguay, Los Angeles, CA, *Chairperson*
James M. Bell, Canaan, NY
Harlow Donald Dunton, New York, NY
Joseph Fischhoff, Detroit, MI
Joseph M. Green, Madison, WI
John F. McDermott, Jr., Honolulu, HI
David A. Mrazek, Denver, CO
Cynthia R. Pfeffer, White Plains, NY
John Schowalter, New Haven, CT
Theodore Shapiro, New York, NY
Leonore Terr, San Francisco, CA

Committee on College Students

Earle Silber, Chevy Chase, MD, *Chairperson*
Robert L. Arnstein, Hamden, CT
Varda Backus, La Jolla, CA
Harrison P. Eddy, New York, NY
Myron B. Liptzin, Chapel Hill, NC
Malkah Tolpin Notman, Brookline, MA
Gloria C. Onque, Pittsburgh, PA
Elizabeth Aub Reid, Cambridge, MA
Lorraine D. Siggins, New Haven, CT
Tom G. Stauffer, White Plains, NY

Committee on Cultural Psychiatry

Ezra Griffith, New Haven, CT, *Chairperson*
Edward Foulks, New Orleans, LA
Pedro Ruiz, Houston, TX
Ronald Wintrob, Providence, RI
Joe Yamamoto, Los Angeles, CA

Committee on the Family

Herta A. Guttman, Montreal, PQ, *Chairperson*
W. Robert Beavers, Dallas, TX
Ellen M. Berman, Merion, PA
Lee Combrinck-Graham, Evanston, IL

Ira D. Glick, New York, NY
Frederick Gottlieb, Los Angeles, CA
Henry U. Grunebaum, Cambridge, MA
Ann L. Price, Avon, CT
Lyman C. Wynne, Rochester, NY

Committee on Governmental Agencies

Roger Peele, Washington, DC, *Chairperson*
Mark Blotcky, Dallas, TX
James P. Cattell, San Diego, CA
Thomas L. Clannon, San Francisco, CA
Naomi Heller, Washington, DC
John P. D. Shemo, Charlottesville, VA
William W. Van Stone, Washington, DC

Committee on Handicaps

William H. Sack, Portland, OR, *Chairperson*
Norman R. Bernstein, Cambridge, MA
Meyer S. Gunther, Wilmette, IL
Robert Nesheim, Duluth, MN
Betty J. Pfefferbaum, Norman, OK
William A. Sonis, Philadelphia, PA
Margaret L. Stuber, Los Angeles, CA
George Tarjan, Los Angeles, CA
Thomas G. Webster, Washington, DC
Henry H. Work, Bethesda, MD

Committee on Human Sexuality

Bertram H. Schaffner, New York, NY, *Chairperson*
Paul L. Adams, Galveston, TX
Richard Friedman, New York, NY
Peggy Hanley-Hackenbruck, Portland, OR
Johanna A. Hoffman, Scottsdale, AZ
Joan A. Lang, Galveston, TX
Stuart E. Nichols, New York, NY
Harris B. Peck, New Rochelle, NY
* John P. Spiegel, Waltham, MA
Terry S. Stein, East Lansing, MI

* deceased

Committee on International Relations

Vamik D. Volkan, Charlottesville, VA, *Chairperson*
Robert M. Dorn, El Macero, CA
John S. Kafka, Washington, DC
Otto F. Kernberg, White Plains, NY
John E. Mack, Chestnut Hill, MA
Roy W. Menninger, Topeka, KS
Peter A. Olsson, Houston, TX
Rita R. Rogers, Palos Verdes Estates, CA
Stephen B. Shanfield, San Antonio, TX

Committee on Medical Education

Stephen C. Scheiber, Deerfield, IL, *Chairperson*
Charles M. Culver, Hanover, NH
Leah Dickstein, Louisville, KY
Steven L. Dubovsky, Denver, CO
Saul I. Harrison, Torrance, CA
David R. Hawkins, Chicago, IL
Harold I. Lief, Philadelphia, PA
Carol C. Nadelson, Boston, MA
Carolyn B. Robinowitz, Washington, DC
Sidney L. Werkman, Washington, DC
Veva H. Zimmerman, New York, NY

Committee on Mental Health Services

W. Walter Menninger, Topeka, KS, *Chairperson*
Mary Jane England, Roseland, NJ
Robert O. Friedel, Richmond, VA
John M. Hamilton, Columbia, MD
Jose Maria Santiago, Tucson, AZ
Steven S. Sharfstein, Baltimore, MD
Herzl R. Spiro, Milwaukee, WI
William L. Webb, Jr., Hartford, CT
George F. Wilson, Somerville, NJ
Jack A. Wolford, Pittsburgh, PA

Committee on Planning and Marketing

Robert W. Gibson, Towson, MD, *Chairperson*
Allan Beigel, Tucson, AZ
Doyle I. Carson, Dallas, TX

Paul J. Fink, Philadelphia, PA
Robert S. Garber, Longboat Key, FL
Richard K. Goodstein, Belle Mead, NJ
Harvey L. Ruben, New Haven, CT
Melvin Sabshin, Washington, DC
Michael R. Zales, Quechee, VT

Committee on Preventive Psychiatry

Naomi Rae-Grant, London, ON, *Chairperson*
Viola W. Bernard, New York, NY
Stephen Fleck, New Haven, CT
Brian J. McConville, Cincinnati, OH
David R. Offord, Hamilton, Ont.
Morton M. Silverman, Chicago, IL
Warren T. Vaughan, Jr., Portola Valley, CA
Ann Marie Wolf-Schatz, Conshohocken, PA

Committee on Psychiatry and the Community

Kenneth Minkoff, Woburn, MA, *Chairperson*
C. Knight Aldrich, Charlottesville, VA
Stephen Goldfinger, Boston, MA
David G. Greenfield, Guilford, CT
H. Richard Lamb, Los Angeles, CA
John C. Nemiah, Hanover, NH
Rebecca L. Potter, Tucson, AZ
John J. Schwab, Louisville, KY
John A. Talbott, Baltimore, MD
Allan Tasman, Louisville, KY
Charles B. Wilkinson, Kansas City, MO

Committee on Psychiatry and the Law

Joseph Satten, San Francisco, CA, *Chairperson*
Renee L. Binder, San Francisco, CA
J. Richard Ciccone, Rochester, NY
Carl P. Malmquist, Minneapolis, MN
Herbert C. Modlin, Topeka, KS
Jonas R. Rappeport, Baltimore, MD
Phillip J. Resnick, Cleveland, OH
William D. Weitzel, Lexington, KY

Committee on Psychiatry and Religion

Richard C. Lewis, New Haven, CT, *Chairperson*
Naleen N. Andrade, Honolulu, HI
Keith G. Meador, Nashville, TN
Abigail R. Ostow, Belmont, MA
Sally K. Severino, White Plains, NY
Clyde R. Snyder, Fayetteville, NC
Edwin R. Wallace, IV, Augusta, GA

Committee on Psychiatry in Industry

Barrie S. Greiff, Newton, MA, *Chairperson*
Peter L. Brill, Radnor, PA
Duane Q. Hagen, St. Louis, MO
R. Edward Huffman, Asheville, NC
Robert Larsen, San Francisco, CA
David E. Morrison, Palatine, IL
David B. Robbins, Chappaqua, NY
Jay B. Rohrlich, New York, NY
Clarence J. Rowe, St. Paul, MN
Jeffrey L. Speller, Cambridge, MA

Committee on Psychopathology

David A. Adler, Boston, MA, *Chairperson*
Jeffrey Berlant, Boise, ID
John P. Docherty, Nashua, NH
Robert A. Dorwart, Cambridge, MA
Robert E. Drake, Hanover, NH
James M. Ellison, Watertown, MA
Howard H. Goldman, Potomac, MD
Anthony F. Lehman, Baltimore, MD
Kathleen A. Pajer, Pittsburgh, PA
Samuel G. Siris, Glen Oaks, NY

Committee on Public Education

Steven E. Katz, New York, NY, *Chairperson*
Jack W. Bonner, III, Asheville, NC
John Donnelly, Hartford, CT
Jeffrey L. Geller, Worcester, MA
Keith H. Johansen, Dallas, TX
Elise K. Richman, Scarsdale, NY
Boris G. Rifkin, Branford, CT

Andrew E. Slaby, Summit, NJ
Robert A. Solow, Los Angeles, CA
Calvin R. Sumner, Buckhannon, WV

Committee on Research

Robert Cancro, New York, NY, *Chairperson*
Jack A. Grebb, New York, NY
John H. Greist, Madison, WI
Jerry M. Lewis, Dallas, TX
John G. Looney, Durham, NC
Sidney Malitz, New York, NY
Zebulon Taintor, New York, NY

Committee on Social Issues

Ian E. Alger, New York, NY, *Chairperson*
William R. Beardslee, Waban, MA
Judith H. Gold, Halifax, NS
Roderic Gorney, Los Angeles, CA
Martha J. Kirkpatrick, Los Angeles, CA
Perry Ottenberg, Philadelphia, PA
Kendon W. Smith, Pearl River, NY

Committee on Therapeutic Care

Donald W. Hammersley, Washington, DC, *Chairperson*
Bernard Bandler, Cambridge, MA
Thomas E. Curtis, Chapel Hill, NC
Donald C. Fidler, Morgantown, WV
William B. Hunter, III, Albuquerque, NM
Roberto L. Jimenez, San Antonio, TX
Milton Kramer, Cincinnati, OH
Theodore Nadelson, Jamaica Plain, MA
William W. Richards, Anchorage, AK

Committee on Therapy

Alan D. Rosenblatt, La Jolla, CA, *Chairperson*
Gerald Adler, Boston, MA
Jules R. Bemporad, Boston, MA
Eugene B. Feigelson, Brooklyn, NY
Robert Michels, New York, NY
Andrew P. Morrison, Cambridge, MA
William C. Offenkrantz, Carefree, AZ

Contributing Members

Gene Abroms, Ardmore, PA
Carlos C. Alden, Jr., Buffalo, NY
Kenneth Z. Altshuler, Dallas, TX
Francis F. Barnes, Washington, DC
Spencer Bayles, Houston, TX
C. Christian Beels, New York, NY
Elissa P. Benedek, Ann Arbor, MI
Sidney Berman, Washington, DC
H. Keith H. Brodie, Durham, NC
Charles M. Bryant, San Francisco, CA
Ewald W. Busse, Durham, NC
Robert N. Butler, New York, NY
Eugene M. Caffey, Jr., Bowie, MD
Robert J. Campbell, New York, NY
Ian L.W. Clancey, Maitland, ON
Sanford I. Cohen, Coral Gables, FL
James S. Eaton, Jr., Washington, DC
Lloyd C. Elam, Nashville, TN
Joseph T. English, New York, NY
Louis C. English, Pomona, NY
Sherman C. Feinstein, Highland Park, IL
Archie R. Foley, New York, NY
Sidney Furst, Bronx, NY
Henry J. Gault, Highland Park, IL
Alexander Gralnick, Port Chester, NY
Milton Greenblatt, Sylmar, CA
Lawrence F. Greenleigh, Los Angeles, CA
Stanley I. Greenspan, Bethesda, MD
Jon E. Gudeman, Milwaukee, WI
Stanley Hammons, Lexington, KY
William Hetznecker, Merion Station, PA
J. Cotter Hirschberg, Topeka, KS
Johanna A. Hoffman, Scottsdale, AZ
Jay Katz, New Haven, CT
James A. Knight, New Orleans, LA
Othilda M. Krug, Cincinnati, OH
Judith Landau-Stanton, Rochester, NY
Alan I. Levenson, Tucson, AZ
Ruth W. Lidz, Woodbridge, CT
Orlando B. Lightfoot, Boston, MA

Norman L. Loux, Sellersville, PA
Albert J. Lubin, Woodside, CA
John A. MacLeod, Cincinnati, OH
Charles A. Malone, Barrington, RI
Peter A. Martin, Lake Orion, MI
Ake Mattsson, Charlottesville, VA
Alan A. McLean, Gig Harbor, WA
David Mendell, Houston, TX
Mary E. Mercer, Nyack, NY
Derek Miller, Chicago, IL
Richard D. Morrill, Boston, MA
Robert J. Nathan, Philadelphia, PA
Joseph D. Noshpitz, Washington, DC
Mortimer Ostow, Bronx, NY
Bernard L. Pacella, New York, NY
Herbert Pardes, New York, NY
Marvin E. Perkins, Salem, VA
David N. Ratnavale, Bethesda, MD
Richard E. Renneker, Pacific Palisades, CA
W. Donald Ross, Cincinnati, OH
Loren Roth, Pittsburgh, PA
Donald J. Scherl, Brooklyn, NY
Charles Shagass, Philadelphia, PA
Miles F. Shore, Boston, MA
Albert J. Silverman, Ann Arbor, MI
Benson R. Snyder, Cambridge, MA
David A. Soskis, Bala Cynwyd, PA
Jeanne Spurlock, Washington, DC
Brandt F. Steele, Denver, CO
Alan A. Stone, Cambridge, MA
Perry C. Talkington, Dallas, TX
Bryce Templeton, Philadelphia, PA
Prescott W. Thompson, Portland, OR
John A. Turner, San Francisco, CA
Gene L. Usdin, New Orleans, LA
Kenneth N. Vogtsberger, San Antonio, TX
Andrew S. Watson, Ann Arbor, MI
Joseph B. Wheelwright, Kentfield, CA
Robert L. Williams, Houston, TX
Paul Tyler Wilson, Bethesda, MD
Sherwyn M. Woods, Los Angeles, CA
Kent A. Zimmerman, Menlo Park, CA
Howard Zonana, New Haven, CT

Life Members

C. Knight Aldrich, Charlottesville, VA
Robert L. Arnstein, Hamden, CT
Bernard Bandler, Cambridge, MA
Walter E. Barton, Hartland, VT
Viola W. Bernard, New York, NY
Henry W. Brosin, Tucson, AZ
John Donnelly, Hartford, CT
Merrill T. Eaton, Omaha, NE
O. Spurgeon English, Narberth, PA
Stephen Fleck, New Haven, CT
Jerome Frank, Baltimore, MD
Robert S. Garber, Longboat Key, FL
Robert I. Gibson, Towson, MD
Margaret M. Lawrence, Pomona, NY
Jerry M. Lewis, Dallas, TX
Harold I. Lief, Philadelphia, PA
Judd Marmor, Los Angeles, CA
Herbert C. Modlin, Topeka, KS
John C. Nemiah, Hanover, NH
William C. Offenkrantz, Carefree, AZ
Mabel Ross, Sun City, AZ
Julius Schreiber, Washington, DC
Robert E. Switzer, Dunn Loring, VA
George Tarjan, Los Angeles, CA
Jack A. Wolford, Pittsburgh, PA
Henry H. Work, Bethesda, MD

BOARD OF DIRECTORS

Officers

President
Allan Beigel
P.O. Box 43460
Tucson, AZ 85733

President-Elect
Charles Wilkinson
600 E. 22nd Street
Kansas City, MO 64108

Secretary
Doyle I. Carson
Timberlawn Psychiatric Hospital
P.O. Box 151489
Dallas, TX 75315-1489

Treasurer
Jack W. Bonner, III
Highland Hospital
P.O. Box 1101
Asheville, NC 28802

Board Members
Judith Gold
Harvey L. Ruben
Pedro Ruiz
John Schowalter

Past Presidents
*William C. Menninger 1946–51
Jack R. Ewalt 1951–53
Walter E. Barton 1953–55
*Sol W. Ginsburg 1955–57
*Dana L. Farnsworth 1957–59
*Marion E. Kenworthy 1959–61
Henry W. Brosin 1961–63
*Leo H. Bartemeier 1963–65
Robert S. Garber 1965–67
Herbert C. Modlin 1967–69
John Donnelly 1969–71
George Tarjan 1971–73
Judd Marmor 1973–75
John C. Nemiah 1975–77
Jack A. Wolford 1977–79
Robert W. Gibson 1979–81
*Jack Weinberg 1981–82
Henry H. Work 1982–85
Michael R. Zales 1985–87
Jerry M. Lewis 1987–89
Carolyn B. Robinowitz 1989–91

*deceased

CONTRIBUTORS

Abbott Laboratories
American Charitable Fund
Dr. and Mrs. Richard Aron
Mr. Robert C. Baker
Maurice Falk Medical Fund
Mrs. Carol Gold
Grove Foundation, Inc.
Miss Gayle Groves
Ittleson Foundation, Inc.
Mr. Barry Jacobson
Mrs. Allan H. Kalmus
Marion E. Kenworthy—Sarah H. Swift Foundation, Inc.
Mr. Larry Korman
McNeil Pharmaceutical
Phillips Foundation
Sandoz, Inc.
Smith Kline Beckman Corporation
Tappanz Foundation, Inc.
The Upjohn Company
van Ameringen Foundation, Inc.
Wyeth Laboratories
Mr. and Mrs. William A. Zales

Index